WRITERS AND CRITICS

Chief Editor

A. NORMAN JEFFARES

Advisory Editors

DAVID DAICHES

C. P. SNOW

A full knowledge of Eliot is compulsory for anyone interested in contemporary literature, and this book assumes that whether Eliot is liked or disliked is of no importance, but that he must be read. The author attempts to give the central facts about Eliot, as a man of letters, as critic, as satirical poet and as devotional poet and dramatist. He is therefore concerned with the structure of Eliot's work, taking as precept Blake's remark that an intellectually honest man changes his opinions but not his principles. He considers this so true that it is possible to approach Eliot's thought and imagery as a consistent unit.

Professor Northrop Frye is Principal of Victoria College in the University of Toronto. A distinguished scholar, literary critic and administrator, he has written *Fearful Symmetry: A Study of William Blake* and *An Anatomy of Criticism*.

T. S. ELIOT

NORTHROP FRYE

CAPRICORN BOOKS
NEW YORK

Published by arrangement with

OLIVER AND BOYD LTD
Tweeddale Court
Edinburgh 1

Copyright © 1963 Text and Bibliography
Northrop Frye

First published 1963

Reprinted 1965
Revised 1968

CAPRICORN BOOKS EDITION 1972

SBN: 399-50263-7

Library of Congress Catalog Card Number:
72-81098

CONTENTS

ACKNOWLEDGMENTS

For permission to quote from T. S. Eliot's works acknowledgment is due to Faber & Faber Ltd and Harcourt, Brace & World, Inc.

The photograph on the front cover is reproduced by permission of Radio Times Hulton Picture Library.

I am greatly indebted to my colleague Miss Jay Macpherson for preparing the Bibliography and for much helpful advice on the text.

N.F.

ABBREVIATED TITLES USED
IN REFERENCES

A.S.G.	=	*After Strange Gods.*
F.L.A.	=	*For Lancelot Andrewes.*
I.C.S.	=	*The Idea of a Christian Society.*
N.D.C.	=	*Notes Towards a Definition of Culture.*
O.P.P.	=	*On Poetry and Poets.*
S.E.	=	*Selected Essays* (1951 edition).
S.W.	=	*The Sacred Wood.*
U.P.U.C.	=	*The Use of Poetry and the Use of Criticism.*

Secondary sources are cited by the author's last name, the full reference being in the Bibliography.

A few of the longer titles have been abbreviated in the text; thus "Prufrock" for "The Love Song of J. Alfred Prufrock," etc.

CHAPTER I

INTRODUCTION

Thomas Stearns Eliot was born in St Louis, Missouri, on 26 Sept. 1888. His father was in business there, and his grandfather was a Unitarian minister who had much to do with the establishing of Washington University in St Louis. His mother was also a writer, and her dramatic poem on Savonarola, edited by her son, indicates an early source of Eliot's interest in poetic drama. The Eliot family had come in the seventeenth century to New England, and for many reasons it was natural that Eliot should go to New England for his university education. He entered Harvard in 1906, when Charles William Eliot was president, a distant relative but, as some glancing references make clear, not intellectually a very congenial figure to his namesake. Eliot wrote poetry at Harvard, but was not especially precocious as a poet. He developed an interest in philosophy that might have made him a distinguished philosopher if he had chosen an academic career. He was caught up in the widespread interest in Oriental philosophy at Harvard, and tells us that he was stopped from going further into it by a fear of losing his sense of participation in the Western tradition.[1] William James was a great name at Harvard, but psychology and pragmatism have had little appeal for Eliot, including the psychological criticism in the tradition of Sainte-Beuve. It may be significant that Eliot's doctoral thesis (accepted, but not presented for the degree, and recently published) was on F. H. Bradley, who represented a very different tradition of philosophical thought.

A travelling fellowship took Eliot to Germany in 1914,

and it was eighteen years before he returned to America. In the fall he entered Merton College, Oxford, to read philosophy. He had earlier discovered the French *symboliste* poets, more particularly Laforgue, and had learned from them how to apply the language of poetry to contemporary life. "The kind of poetry that I needed," he says, "to teach me the use of my own voice, did not exist in English at all; it was only to be found in French."[2] He learned much from the chief English study of these poets, Arthur Symons' *The Symbolist Movement in Literature*. His first major poem, "The Love Song of J. Alfred Prufrock," completed in 1911, appeared in 1915 in *Poetry*, a magazine recently founded in Chicago, and a main outlet for the stream of new American poetry of which Eliot's work formed part. In the same year (1915) he married and settled in England. He had met Ezra Pound in 1914, and later met Wyndham Lewis and James Joyce, contributing also to the magazines and anthologies that Pound's driving energy was establishing. His first prose work to appear was an essay on Pound published anonymously in America in 1917. *Prufrock and Other Observations* was also published in 1917, showing the influence of Laforgue most markedly in the lunar symbolism and the use of ironic dialogue. In 1919 a second group of poems appeared, and in the same year a collection of the two books, called at first *Ara Vos Prec* and then simply *Poems* (1920). With this volume Eliot's early poetry was virtually complete.

A collection of early essays called *The Sacred Wood*, and including "Tradition and the Individual Talent," which outlined his "impersonal" theory of the poetic process, appeared also in 1920. Although Eliot's general position, "Classical in literature, royalist in politics, anglo-catholic in religion," was not announced until the preface to *For Lancelot Andrewes* in 1928, it was clear that their opposites, Romanticism, "Whiggery," and secularism, were already in the intellectual doghouse. There followed three influential essays on Marvell, Dryden and the meta-physical poets (*Homage to John Dryden*, 1924). In 1922 Eliot began his own periodical, *Criterion*, which he edited until 1939, the purpose of which was, he tells us, to create a place for the new attitudes to literature and criticism, and to make English letters a part of the European cultural community.[3]

The first issue of *Criterion* carried *The Waste Land*, a long poem that Eliot had been working on for some time. In its original form it is said to have run to over eight hundred lines, then in consultation with Ezra Pound, who was accustomed to editing other poets with the greatest confidence, it was cut to its present length. No doubt most readers of Eliot would prefer to have the original version, but it is possible that Pound's editing improved the poem, and very probable that it made it more enigmatic. The poem is dedicated to Pound as "il miglior fabbro," a phrase from Dante used as a chapter heading in Pound's *Spirit of Romance*. With this poem and its successor *The Hollow Men* (1925), Eliot found himself, somewhat to his chagrin, the spokesman of a post-war attitude which found in his waste-land imagery an "objective correlative" (of which more later), for its disillusionment, or what Eliot calls its illusion of being disillusioned.[4]

For such readers it was a shock when Eliot, after becoming a naturalised British subject and joining the Church of England in 1927, announced the position already quoted in *For Lancelot Andrews*, but, on the whole, the new attitude was consistent enough with the earlier one, only the content being changed. Still, the change of content did turn Eliot from a satiric to a devotional poet, a practising Anglo-Catholic layman ready to write a verse play for a campaign to build new churches (*The Rock*, 1934), or to charge a heavy brigade of irony at the religiously light-minded:

And on Easter Day, we couldn't get to the country,
So we took young Cyril to church.

Eliot joined the publishing house of Faber and Gwyer, later Faber and Faber, in 1925, and shortly became a director. He returned to the United States in 1932 as Professor of Poetry at Harvard, in which office he delivered the lectures called *The Use of Poetry and the Use of Criticism*. These were followed by a more doctrinaire series given at Virginia in 1933 and published as *After Strange Gods*, ominously subtitled "A Primer of Modern Heresy." During the nineteen-thirties Eliot's critical writing became increasingly concerned with what he calls "the struggle against Liberalism." His later social criticism is represented by two essays, *The Idea of a Christian Society* (1940) and *Notes Towards a Definition of Culture* (1948), the former especially reflecting much of the spirit of that miserable time between Munich and Dunkirk.

It was mainly during the nineteen-thirties that Eliot completed *Four Quartets*, the culmination of his non-dramatic poetry. The last Quartet, "Little Gidding," takes us up to the time when the Nazi bombs were falling in London. Meanwhile his interest in drama, which had begun with *Sweeney Agonistes* (1927) and continued in *The Rock*, had led to the writing of *Murder in the Cathedral* (1935), a tragedy on the murder of Becket, and *The Family Reunion* (1939), with a country-house setting in which the Furies of Aeschylus make a disconcerting, and, according to Eliot, unstageable appearance.[5]

After the war Eliot continued to live in England, with occasional visits to America. He wrote relatively little non-dramatic poetry in his later years, apart from a collection of children's verse, reminiscent of Edward Lear, *Old Possum's Book of Practical Cats* (1939). "Possum" is a nickname for Eliot, occurring in Pound's *Cantoes*. He returned to drama with the tragicomedy *The Cocktail*

Party (1949), perhaps the most commercially successful of all his plays. This was followed by two other comedies, *The Confidential Clerk* (1953) and *The Elder Statesman* (1958). Both were produced at the Edinburgh Festival and have had good runs, but have never equalled the popularity of their predecessors. There was also a steady series of critical essays, most of them, as one would expect with an established writer, lectures given on special occasions. Many of these were collected in a volume called *On Poetry and Poets* (1956). In 1948 Eliot received two of the greatest honours a contemporary writer can obtain, the Order of Merit and the Nobel Prize for Literature, and a few years later the Hanseatic Goethe Prize. In 1947 his wife, who had been ill for some time, died and in 1957 he married Valerie Fletcher, to whom *On Poetry and Poets* and *The Elder Statesman* are dedicated. He died in early January of 1965.

Eliot's poems and plays have each been collected in a single volume, and the reader of Eliot will also find essential *Selected Essays* and a posthumous collection, *To Criticize the Critic*, besides the other critical works referred to above. Even these do not contain everything that a student of Eliot would want, as there are still many uncollected and fugitive pieces, and many prefaces to books. The present book, by policy, avoids referring to any writing of Eliot not readily accessible to the ordinary reader.

A thorough knowledge of Eliot is compulsory for anyone interested in contemporary literature. Whether he is liked or disliked is of no importance, but he must be read. So much is assumed by the present book: further value-judgments and estimates of comparative greatness are the concern of the reader. The literature on Eliot is enormous, and the present addition to it is an elementary handbook, claiming no originality beyond that of arrangement. Blake remarks that an intellectually honest man changes his opinions but not his principles, and this is so true of Eliot that it is possible to approach him deductively, treating the structure of his thought and imagery as a consistent unit. Such an approach saves a good deal of space without being misleading. In dealing with the poetry I have tried to emphasise the structure and to avoid getting lost in the allusions.

Almost every major poet has expressed certain social and intellectual attitudes which may be essential to the understanding of his poetry but are often unacceptable to many of his readers. This is no less true of Eliot than it is of Yeats or Pound or Whitman or Hopkins. It is, or should be, a central principle of criticism that no major poet stands or falls by his views, however closely they may be identified with his creative work. If I begin with what seem the clichés of hostility to Eliot, passages from *After Strange Gods* and the like, it is for the purpose of defining, as quickly as possible, what must be considered but can also be clearly separated from Eliot's permanent achievement, leaving that achievement intact.

REFERENCES

1. *A.S.G.* p. 40.
2. "Yeats," *O.P.P.* p. 252.
3. *N.D.C.* p. 117.
4. "Thoughts After Lambeth," *S.E.* p. 368.
5. "Poetry and Drama," *O.P.P.* p. 84.

CHAPTER II

ANTIQUE DRUM

An American moving to Europe to live is likely to become more sharply aware of the "Western" context and origin of his cultural tradition, and hence to be attracted to some theory about the shape and development of that tradition. Such theories fall into two main groups, the going-up and the going-down. The going-up one started as the humanistic view, predominant from the sixteenth to the eighteenth century and implied in the title of Gibbon's *Decline and Fall*. This is a U-shaped parabola reaching its bottom with the "triumph of barbarism and religion" in the Dark Ages, and moving upward with the revival of learning. Not only Gibbon but the deeply conservative Johnson assumed a steady improvement of life and manners up to his time, an assumption which Eliot regards as a major source of Johnson's strength and security as a critic. The complementary or Romantic view is an inverted U rising to its height in medieval "Gothic" and falling off with the Renaissance, and is most articulate in Ruskin.

In the late nineteenth century the going-up parabola lost its opening curve and developed into a theory of progress, which Darwin's theory of evolution was supposed to confirm scientifically. The key to progress was the growing respect for individual freedom, making for democracy in politics, and liberalism, with a strong affinity to Protestantism, in thought. The descendant of the Ruskinian view we may call, in an image of *The Waste Land*, the bobsled or "down we went" theory. According to this, the height of civilisation was reached in the Middle Ages, when society, religion and the arts expressed a common set of standards and values. This does not mean that living conditions were better then— a point which could hardly matter less—but that the cultural synthesis of the Middle Ages symbolises an ideal of European community. All history since represents a degeneration of this ideal. Christendom breaks down into nations, the Church into heresies and sects, knowledge into specialisations, and the end of the process is what the writer is sorrowfully contemplating in his own time: "the disintegration of Christendom, the decay of a common belief and a common culture."[1]

This view, though held as far on the left as William Morris, is more congenial to such Catholic apologists as Chesterton, and to such literary critics as Ezra Pound, whose conception of "usura" sums up a good deal of its demonology. Eliot's social criticism, and much of his literary criticism, falls within this framework. He is uniformly opposed to theories of progress that invoke the authority of evolution, and contemptuous of writers who attempt to popularise a progressive view, like H. G. Wells. The "disintegration" of Europe began soon after Dante's time; a "diminution" of all aspects of culture has afflicted England since Queen Anne; the nineteenth century was an age of progressive "degradation"; in the last fifty years evidences of "decline" are visible in every department of human activity. Eliot adopts, too, the rhetorical device, found in Newman and others, of asserting that "There are two and only two finally tenable hypotheses about life: the Catholic and the materialistic."[2] Everything which is neither, including Protestantism, "Whiggery," liberalism and humanism, is in between, and consequently forms a series of queasy transitional hesitations, each worse than the one before it.

We are reminded of Spengler's *Decline of the West*, a best-seller in Germany when Eliot was writing *The*

Waste Land, which sees history as a series of cultures that behave like organisms, so that their decline is an inevitable ageing process. Eliot could doubtless take only the lowest view of Spengler's book, but Spengler's is the most coherent statement of the theory of Western decline, and any writer who adopts a version of that theory gets involved in Spenglerian metaphors. Thus Eliot falls into such phrases as "an age of immaturity or an age of senility," utters prophecies about "the dark ages before us" and "the barbarian nomads of the future," and incorporates references to blood and soil in his otherwise very un-Teutonic vocabulary.

Eliot belonged to one of the great dynastic New England families who have supplied so much cultural and political leadership in American life, and, like other American writers with such names as Adams and Lowell, reflects the preoccupations of an unacknowledged aristocracy, preoccupations with tradition, with breeding, with the loss of common social assumptions. "The mind resorts to reason for want of training," said Henry Adams, and Adams felt that man could worship only "silent and infinite force," either in the spiritual form of the Virgin of Chartres or in the material form of the dynamo—a close parallel to Eliot's dialectic. Eliot feels that man's natural society is not classless, but one in which "an aristocracy should have a peculiar and essential function."[3] A functional aristocracy implies a functional peasantry. The small regional community, homogeneous in race and preferably in language, is the proper cultural unit. We are even told that "it would appear to be for the best that the great majority of human beings should go on living in the place in which they were born."[4] In the essays on culture and Christian society much attention is paid to Welsh and Scottish cultural nationalism as a "safeguard" against the tendency "to lose their racial character." In *After Strange Gods* Eliot, addressing a Virginian audience, expresses sympathy with the con-

servative neo-agrarian movement of Southern intellec-
tuals, and remarks: "I think that the chances for the re-
establishment of a native culture are perhaps better here
than in New England. You are farther away from New
York; you have been less industrialised and less invaded
by foreign races; and you have a more opulent soil."

In the poetry the mingling of races and the sense of
lost pedigree symbolise a disintegration of culture, like
the ethnical miscellany in "Gerontion" and the woman
in *The Waste Land* who claims to be "echt deutsch" because she comes from Lithuania. A more squalid mon-
grelism may be represented by Sam Wauchope in
Sweeney Agonistes, whom his American friends boast to be
"a real live Britisher," but who appears to be nothing
more than a Canadian. In "Gerontion" and elsewhere
the Jew embodies the rootlessness of the modern metro-
polis, and Virginia, with a different problem on its
hands, is informed that "reasons of race and religion
combine to make any large number of free-thinking
Jews undesirable." Behind this is a belief that "blood
kinship" and attachment to the soil are features of a
"harmony with nature" which a genuine society has,
"unintelligible to the industrialized mind."[5]

These features of Eliot's thought are well known,
widely criticised, and for most readers fantastic or repel-
lent. It is therefore important to realise that the historical
myth behind them is not essential to his real argument.
The real decline is from an ideal which may be symbolised by medieval culture, but remains in the present
to condemn and challenge the contemporary world.
Thus the historical myth is projected from a conception
of two levels of human life which are always simultaneously present.

All views of life that Eliot would call serious or mature
distinguish between two selves in man: the selfish and the
self-respecting. These are not only distinguishable but
opposed, and in Christianity the opposition is total, as for

it the selfish self is to be annihilated, and the other is the immortal soul one is trying to save. Theories of conduct exalting the freedom of the personality or character without making this distinction are disastrous. They lead to a breakdown of community, for the ordinary or selfish self is locked in its private jail-cell, "each in his prison," its only relation to society being an aggressive or acquisitive one. The argument of *After Strange Gods* leads up to and concludes with an attack on the undiscriminating theory of personality. What is admired in modern culture "tends naturally to be the *unregenerate* personality." We thus have a lower level of ordinary or mere personality, or what we shall loosely call the ego, and the higher level of the genuine self. The ordinary personality is Rousseau's noble savage: it regards the community as a limitation of its freedom, and judges the community according to the amount of inconvenience to the ego that it causes. Eliot starts from Burke's view that society is prior to the individual. As Burke says, art is man's nature: the human world is a civilised one, an order of nature distinct from the physical world. Laws for the will, beliefs for the reason, and great classics of culture for the imagination, are there from the beginning. If a man is a twentieth-century Englishman, he cannot claim that he is a timeless and spaceless "I": his context cannot be separated from his real personality, which it completes and fulfils.

The particular continuum into which an individual is born, Eliot calls his culture or tradition. By culture Eliot means "that which makes life worth living":[6] one's total way of life, including art and education, but also cooking and sports. By tradition, also, Eliot means both a conscious and an unconscious life in a social continuum. "What I mean by tradition involves all those habitual actions, habits and customs ... which represent the blood kinship of 'the same people living in the same place.' "[7] The significance of the phrase "blood kinship"

we have already commented on. Political life may become world-wide and depersonalised, but culture, in
poetry and painting as in fine wines, demands locality,
a realised environment. Eliot stresses the feeling for soil
and local community in his essays on Virgil and Kipling,
two poets who have little in common except a popular
reputation for being imperialists.

In Matthew Arnold's conception of culture, religion is
a cultural product, a part of which culture is the whole;
hence the human value of a religion lies mainly in the
quality of its worldliness. In Eliot religion forms a third
level above human society. Its presence there guarantees
Burke's distinction between a higher order of human and
a lower order of physical nature. "If this 'supernatural' is
suppressed . . . the *dualism* of man and nature collapses at
once. Man is man because he can recognize supernatural
realities, not because he can invent them."[8] Hence
human culture is aligned with a spiritual reality which is
superior to it and yet within it, the kind of relationship
represented in Christianity by the Incarnation. Eliot
stresses the importance of this conception when he speaks
of culture metaphorically as the "incarnation" of a
religion, the human manifestation of a superhuman
reality. A culture's religion "should mean for the individual and for the group something toward which they
strive, not merely something which they possess,"[9] and it
demonstrates that "the natural life and the supernatural
life have a conformity to each other which neither has
with the mechanistic life."[10] In *After Strange Gods* Eliot
uses "orthodoxy" to mean a conscious and voluntary
commitment to the religious aspect of tradition. No culture which repudiates religion and deifies itself, like
Marxist Communism, can get man out of the squirrel-
cage of the ego, though it may "on its own level" give
"an apparent meaning to life."[11]

The genuine personality, then, is concrete man, man
in the context of certain social institutions, whether

nation, church, culture or social class. The ego or ordinary personality is an abstraction, and a parasitic by-product of the genuine personality; it is anti-cultural and anti-traditional. But as the ego is not the genuine self, it is really sub-human.

> The lengthened shadow of a man
> Is history, said Emerson,
> Who had not seen the silhouette
> Of Sweeney straddled in the sun.

What Emerson said was: "An institution is the lengthened shadow of a man." In Eliot the reverse is true: the natural man or ego is the shadow of an institution, or man in genuine society. Swift's Yahoo is pure natural man, what man would be without institutions. Eliot's Sweeney is not a Yahoo, but his "silhouette" reminds us of one. At the end of his essay on Baudelaire, Eliot quotes T. E. Hulme as saying that institutions are necessary because man is essentially bad.

An authoritarian inference from original sin is not very logical, for those entrusted with imposing social discipline on others cannot by hypothesis be any better themselves. Eliot does not say that he approves of what Hulme says, but only that Baudelaire would have done so. But still Eliot thinks of democracy as permeated by the natural man's admiration for himself. What the natural man wants is only generic: food, houses, sexual intercourse and possessions, and a society which accepts these wants as genuine social ends becomes totalitarian. Fascism and Communism are the products of strong tendencies within democracy itself, and our horror at these products springs from the ego's dislike of inconvenience rather than love of freedom. Eliot makes much of the virtue of humility, which he says in "East Coker" provides "The only wisdom we can hope to acquire." Humility is the opposite of pride, traditionally the essence of sin, and pride is life centered in the ego. The "proud" attitude to social evils is to regard them as wholly external to oneself, for oneself, in a state of pride, is not to be examined, much less condemned. It ascribes everything it dislikes to an economic system or political party, expects miraculous results from a transfer of power, and is always in a revolutionary attitude.

Tradition for Eliot is far from being a cult of doing what has been done before. "Humility" is also a prerequisite of originality. The self-expression that springs from pride is more egocentric, but less individual, for the only self that can get expressed in this way is one just like everyone else. "Cousin Nancy" smokes and dances and impresses her aunts as modern, and fulfils "Waldo" Emerson's doctrine of self-reliance and "Matthew" Arnold's individualised culture, but what she does is still only fashionable conformity. The last line of this poem is quoted from Meredith's sonnet on the hopeless rebellion of Lucifer, and aligns Nancy with the same futility.

For most people acceptance of culture and tradition is unconscious, expressed in assumption and prejudice. A man is hardly a human being at all until he has entered a tradition, or what some call a social contract. But "What is important is a structure of society in which there will be, from 'top' to 'bottom,' a continuous gradation of cultural levels . . . we should not consider the upper levels as possessing *more* culture than the lower, but as representing a more conscious culture and a greater specialization of culture."[12] There should be, therefore, an "élite" of those for whom culture and tradition have become conscious. They include poets for at least two reasons. First, "poetry differs from every other art in having a value for the people of the poet's race and language, which it can have for no other." Second, "unless we have those few men who combine an exceptional sensibility with an exceptional power over words, our own ability, not merely to express, but even to feel any but the crudest emotions, will degenerate."[13] They also include critics, who depend on "a settled society" "in which the difference of religious and political views are not extreme."[14] This last implies that the élite should have a close connexion with the culture's religion.

Religion sees human life in relation to superhuman life, as a kind of continuous imitation of it. This is expressed in certain acts, or sacraments, and in certain forms of thought, or dogmas derived from revelation. Religion cannot be identical with culture, except in the City of God or in a very primitive society;[15] but if religion and culture draw apart, society loses its sense of direction, and the élite and the unreflecting masses become unintelligible to each other. Eliot's conception of religion is thus a sacramental and Catholic one: the Church is the definitive form of ritual and faith, and the essence of religion is participation in the Church. Protestant conceptions of the church would doubtless not be admissible to Eliot if we could suppose he knew what they were. When he says "the life of Protestantism depends upon the survival of that against which it protests,"[16] we are apparently to take this lugubrious pun as representing his understanding of the faith that the head of his church defends.

Eliot's "élite" are interpreters of their society, and show that what is most deliberately and consciously cultured in any society is also central to it, and guides its main current. Eliot, like Arnold, feels that "the dissentients must remain marginal,"[17] even when they form the majority. For Eliot admits, even stresses, that we can have an *Athanasius contra mundum* situation in which "the man who is 'representative' of his time may be in opposition to the most widely-accepted beliefs of his time."[18] If Athanasius is right, he is in the "centre" of his society; if he is wrong or partly right, he is "marginal." Neither Eliot nor Arnold has explored the difficulties in this metaphor very far. Eliot's élite is similar, as he recognises, to Coleridge's "clerisy," but Eliot's argument is more pro-Catholic, stressing the importance of contemplative orders in the church. Coleridge's differences from him on these points "now sound merely quaint."[19] In Eliot, as again in Arnold, the Establishment is society's recognition both of the centrality of the church and of the distinction between the church and the marginal sects. Of disestablishment Eliot says: "the risks are so great that such an act can be nothing but a desperate measure"[20]—a strong statement for a poet brought up in the United States.

It follows that education should have the socially engaged personality as its goal. One type of education, distinguished by Eliot as instruction or information, is designed to provide the ego with extended powers. This type usually depends on a socially subversive theory aiming at transforming society by equality of opportunity. The fable of the belly and members is replaced in Eliot by an analogy of the head and trunk of the body politic. We feel that we are members of one body when the culture of a minority is the conscious form of the culture of the majority. Education should aim at a social ideal like Newman's gentleman, whose leisure and good taste are produced by an awareness of social context rather than by class privilege or private enterprise. Arnold's conception of culture is evaluative, the *best* that has been thought and said, and as such plays a revolutionary role in society. "Culture seeks to do away with classes," and the permeation of society by culture tends toward equality. In Eliot the conception of culture is descriptive, hence it plays no revolutionary role. The classes of the past may give place to the élites of the future, but culture itself does nothing to disturb the class structure.

Eliot's literary criticism falls into two parts, a literary polemic derived from the myth of decline and a critical theory derived from the study and practice of literature. The former is what concerns us here.

The progressive view of history produced the post-Romantic conception of English literature which Eliot challenged. According to this, originality in poetry is an aspect of individual freedom in life; hence Shakespeare, who drew individuals so well, and Milton, a Protestant revolutionary, express the real genius of English literature. The era from Dryden to Johnson was an inferior and prosier age, but the Romantic movement re-established the main tradition, which continued in Britain through Tennyson and Swinburne, and in America through Whitman's conception of poetry as self-expression.

Eliot's historical view of English literature is a point-for-point reversal of the progressive one. The post-Romantic conception of "personality," failing to distinguish the craftsman from the ordinary personality, assumes that the former is the medium or vehicle of the latter, instead of the other way round. In "Tradition and the Individual Talent" Eliot speaks of the poetic process as "impersonal," not an expression of personality but an "escape" from it. The poet's mind is a place where something happens to words, like a catalyser which accompanies but does not manipulate a chemical action. In other early essays, though Eliot agrees with Arnold about the immaturity of the Romantic poets, he means by "Romanticism" chiefly the popular post-Romantic residue of their influence which is contemporary with himself. This Romanticism, he says, "leads its disciples only back upon themselves."[21] Romanticism, then, as a creative process emanating from and returning to the ego, occupies the foreground of Eliot's historical dialectic, the contemporary world at the bottom of the Western mountain, as far as we can get from the "anti-romantic" "practical sense of realities" in Dante's *Vita Nuova*.[22]

The First World War discredited the view that the northern, liberal, largely Protestant cultures of England and Germany were, with America, the architects of a

new world. Latin and Catholic Europe began to look
like a cultural as well as a political ally. The essay on
Blake in *The Sacred Wood* is full of anti-Nordic mythology:
Blake's prophecies "illustrate the crankiness, the
eccentricity, which frequently affects writers outside of
the Latin tradition." So although Eliot's view of literature is "classical," his Classicism regards Latin medieval
culture, and Dante in particular, as the culmination of the
Classical achievement. Dante's greatness is partly a product of a time when Europe "was mentally more united
than we can now conceive." At such a time literature
achieves its greatest power and clarity: "there is an
opacity, or inspissation of poetic style throughout
Europe after the Renaissance." So Eliot explicitly pre-
fers the culture which produced Dante to that which
produced Shakespeare.[23]

Eliot reiterates that Shakespeare is as great a poet as
Dante, but, reflecting an age nearer ours, the materials
out of which his poetry is made are shoddier. "Dante
made great poetry out of a great philosophy of life; and
Shakespeare made equally great poetry out of an inferior and muddled philosophy of life."[24] Eliot, like Shaw,
finds Shakespeare's philosophy of life a mass of platitudes
with a pessimistic slant, and agrees with Archer that
Elizabethan drama is an "impure art," though his moral
is the opposite of Archer's belief in "progress . . . and in
the superiority and efficiency of the present age."[25] He
also agrees with Arnold that Shakespeare is too clever
to have a good effect on tradition. "If you try to imitate
Shakespeare you will certainly produce a series of stilted,
forced, and violent distortions of language."[26] The
conclusion is that we should admire Shakespeare, but not
for liberal or Romantic reasons. Shakespeare does not
always take a maturely dim view of human nature: his
rhetoric may yield to his hero's desire to "see himself in
a dramatic light," as Othello does in his Aleppo speech,
where he shows a lack of humility. We are told that

Hamlet, the Bible of the Romantics, is "most certainly an artistic failure," and (in two grinning footnotes) that Rymer, the seventeenth-century critic who called *Othello* a bloody farce, "makes out a very good case."

The reader may be confused by the suggestion that Shakespeare made his poetry "out of" a philosophy, whether profound or what Eliot calls "ragbag." Eliot establishes three main philosophical connexions with Shakespeare, the Cerberus of the modern world raising its heads. The ancestor of modern sceptical liberalism is Montaigne, to whom Shakespeare owed much (here Eliot may have been over-influenced by J. M. Robertson, as he was in his *Hamlet* essay by Robertson's disintegrating fantasies). The ancestor of Romantic egoism is Seneca the Stoic, whose conception of the hero seems like a cult of spiritual pride. The ancestry of the secularism that ends in expediency is in the cynical political views ascribed by the Elizabethans to Machiavelli. Machiavelli himself said that unscrupulousness in politics is necessary because men are "ungrateful, fickle, false, cowards, covetous," which sounds like a belief in original sin, hence "In Machiavelli there is no cynicism whatever."[27]

Eliot's political attitude is said in the preface to *For Lancelot Andrewes* to be "royalist." Royalism for Eliot, as for Burke, could well mean the maintaining of a symbol of continuity in society clear of party politics or class struggle. But though Eliot announced an *Outline of Royalism* and speaks of the divine right of kings as a "noble faith,"[28] the conception has little importance in his work except as an indication that he was taking a side in the seventeenth-century civil war. Much of Eliot's criticism revolves around the first part of the seventeenth century, a period he approaches as one which contains in embryo all the disintegrating tendencies of our time. Shakespeare, Tourneur and Jonson can still control them while reflecting them, but Massinger and Ford are beginning to yield to them. Then came the Civil War, the

Puritan emigrations, including the Eliots from East Coker, the closing of the theatres, the overthrow of everything catholic in the Church of England from the Little Gidding community to Archbishop Laud, and the poetry of Milton. With all this the tradition of English culture fell to pieces, and the modern world was born. For anyone concerned to oppose the tendencies of that world, "the Civil War is not ended,"[29] as Eliot was still insisting as late as 1947.

Milton was a poet of the devil's party and at least the devil probably knew it. He subjected the language to a deterioration which meant that on later writing his influence could only be for the worse. He built a "Chinese wall" across poetry, the work of a man imaginatively as well as physically blind, showing a vague visual sense and leading nowhere "outside of the mazes of sound." His rhetoric is that of "the greatest of all eccentrics," valid only for Milton himself, an apotheosis of the ego. It is full of tricks like "the facile use of resonant names" which Marlowe outgrew, and Marlowe's Mephistopheles "renders Milton's Satan superfluous." Johnson was right in finding *Lycidas* full of "absurdities"; *L'Allegro* and *Il Penseroso* are on a level with "the lighter and less successful poems of Keats"; Swinburne is praised for abusing *Comus*, which is also called "the death of the masque."

With Dryden the real tradition was to some degree reestablished, for it is "easier to get back to healthy language from Dryden." Though Eliot admires Pope and does what he can to rehabilitate Dryden and Johnson as poets and critics, he does not maintain that the Augustan age produced a poet of the stature of, say, Racine in France. Of the Romantics, those who best illustrate the egocentric quality of Romanticism are Byron and Shelley. The fact that Shelley, as a man, was "self-centred, and sometimes almost a blackguard" is relevant, because although "Wordsworth does not present a very pleasing personality either," Shelley's "abuse of poetry" is greater. Byron's egoism is connected with the "defective sensibility" which made him write English like a dead language. Blake's work is egocentric because it contains a philosophy which Blake thought out himself instead of borrowing from his tradition. In reputation the biggest figure in this period is Goethe, and Goethe "dabbled in both philosophy and poetry and made no great success of either."[30]

Contemporary literature is of course full of the detritus of Romanticism. "Religion and Literature," an essay unlikely ever to rank with *Areopagitica* as a ringing manifesto of intellectual freedom, says that "while individual modern writers of eminence can be improving, contemporary literature as a whole tends to be degrading." Hardy is "a powerful personality uncurbed by any institutional attachment," who expressed that personality without having anything "particularly wholesome or edifying" to express. D. H. Lawrence's "vision is spiritual, but spiritually sick."[31] Yeats, with his little-Ireland folklore and his occultism, has a minor and peripheral mythology. (So did the Hebrew prophets and Christian apostles, but, as explained above, they were really central, because right.) Elsewhere we find slighting references to Bernard Shaw, H. G. Wells, and Bertrand Russell. These are prose writers, and "good prose cannot be written by a people without convictions."[32] What convictions they are also seems to be important. Our attention is called "to the great excellence of Bishop Hensley Henson's prose," but we are told that Russell, in his quasi-Stoical *A Free Man's Worship*, wrote "bad prose."[33]

"We all agree about the 'cultural breakdown',"[34] says Eliot, but myths of decline usually have a codicil: the writer has something contemporary to recommend which promises to arrest the decline of civilisation. Eliot himself points out that his historical dialectic, on its literary side,

is attached to a tactical campaign to get new types of
writing recognised.[35] Of the writers he defends, Ezra
Pound and James Joyce are the most prominent.
Romantic, Protestant and liberal tendencies in the
English tradition make it more culturally schismatic
than the French tradition, where Racine and Baudelaire
"are in some ways more like each other than they are like
anyone else,"[36] and which is closer to the Latin centre of
European culture. It is significant that Pound and Joyce
reflect the influence of Latin and Catholic civilisation,
and significant too that their cultural conservatism seems
to go with originality of expression. The discovery, with
the belated publication of the poetry of Hopkins, that the
most disturbingly original Victorian poet was a Jesuit
priest looked like confirmation of the same principle, but
in *After Strange Gods* Eliot refuses to play this ace and
finesses with Joyce, the "most ethically orthodox writer"
of our time.

Eliot's skill in quotation and in setting passages of un-
equal merit beside each other put his handling of his
critical polemic on an unusually high level of objectivity. Only occasionally can we see the rhetorical shad-
ing of the arguments. In the final canto of the *Inferno*
we come upon Dante's Satan, with three heads, one of
which is meditatively chewing Judas Iscariot. The un-
instructed reader might find the scene a trifle barbaric,
and feel that what Milton did with Satan was more
civilised. Eliot, recognising the danger, says: "The vision
of Satan may seem grotesque, especially if we have fixed
in our minds the curly-haired Byronic hero of Milton."
This remark is too remote from Milton to be even misleading: it is sheer polemic and nothing more. In his
essay on Sir John Davies, Eliot sets a passage from
Orchestra beside one from *The Ancient Mariner* containing
the line "His great bright eye most silently," and says
parenthetically that "most" is a blemish. Considering
that *The Ancient Mariner* is a deliberate imitation of ballad

idiom, with its bits of metrical putty, it is perhaps not a blemish. But a sense of the superiority of pre-Romantic craftsmanship has been quietly implanted in the reader's mind.

With the Second World War and the completion of "Little Gidding," the Civil War reached an armistice on its last battlefield. Eliot, Pound and Joyce were by that time established writers. In later essays the polemical tone is abandoned, the Romantics are referred to without much animus, and the terms classic and romantic are now said to belong to "literary politics."[37] A second essay on Milton holds a cautious Geiger counter up to that poet and decides that "at last" it is safe for poets to read him. In pointing out that Milton can hardly have been a worse influence on later epic than Shakespeare on later verse drama, Eliot comes close to saying that every major poet builds a "Chinese wall"—a principle that will in due course be applied to Eliot himself. "That every great work of poetry tends to make impossible the production of equally great works of the same kind is indisputable."[38] The greater urbanity sometimes goes with a loss of incisiveness. "I should myself rate Campion as a more important poet than Herrick, though very much below Herbert" sounds amateurish compared to an earlier statement that the critic's task is to isolate quality, not to determine rank.[39]

The best comment on Eliot's polemic is that of his mentor in "Little Gidding": "These things have served their purpose; let them be." We may consider applying to Eliot his own early comment that Arnold "went for game outside of the literary preserve altogether," which "we must regret," because it "might perhaps have been carried on as effectively, if not quite so neatly, by some disciple (had there been one) in an editorial position on a newspaper."[40] Certainly when we read in *The Idea of a Christian Society*: "It is a matter of concern not only in this country, but has been mentioned with concern by the late Supreme Pontiff . . . that the masses of the people have become increasingly alienated from Christianity," we may wonder if it really needed a writer of Eliot's abilities to produce that sentence. A poet's specific task has something to do with visualising the Promised Land: on the historical level, he may often be a lost leader, a Moses floundering in a legal desert.[41] As Eliot says, it is the Word in the desert that is most likely to hear "The loud lament of the disconsolate chimera." It is difficult to feel that Eliot's view of Western culture is anything more than a heresy in his own sense of the word, a partial insight with "a seductive simplicity" which is "altogether more plausible than the truth."[42] The orthodoxy of which it is a heresy would be, or include, a much larger "truth" about our very complex situation than the mythology of decline affords. Nevertheless, the construct from which Eliot's social criticism is projected is also that of his poetry, hence it illuminates our understanding of his poetry and its relation to his own time.

REFERENCES

1. "What is a Classic?" *O.P.P.* p. 61.
2. "Modern Education and the Classics," *S.E.* p. 514.
3. *N.D.C.* p. 48.
4. *N.D.C.* 52.
5. "Rudyard Kipling," *O.P.P.* p. 250.
6. *N.D.C.* p. 27.
7. *A.S.G.* p. 18.
8. "Second Thoughts About Humanism," *S.E.* p. 485.
9. *N.D.C.* p. 31.
10. *I.C.S.* p. 61.
11. *N.D.C.* p. 34.
12. *N.D.C.* p. 48.
13. "The Social Function of Poetry," *O.P.P.* p. 18, 21.
14. "Johnson as Critic and Poet," *O.P.P.* p. 191.
15. *N.D.C.* p. 67.
16. *N.D.C.* p. 75.
17. *I.C.S.* p. 46.
18. "Goethe as the Sage," *O.P.P.* p. 219.
19. *I.C.S.* p. 35.
20. *I.C.S.* p. 49.
21. "Imperfect Critics," *S.W.*
22. "Dante," *S.E.* p. 275.
23. "Second Thoughts About Humanism," *S.E.* p. 488.

24. Preface to Wilson Knight, *The Wheel of Fire* (1930).

25. "Four Elizabethan Dramatists," *S.E.* pp. 114, 117.

26. "Dante," *S.E.* p. 252.

27. "Niccolo Macchiavelli," *F.L.A.* pp. 49, 52.

28. "John Bramhall," *S.E.* p. 360.

29. "Milton II," *O.P.P.* p. 148.

30. "Shelley and Keats," *U.P.U.C.* p. 99.

31. *A.S.G.* p. 60.

32. *I.C.S.* p. 20.

33. *I.C.S.* p. 79; "The Modern Mind," *U.P.U.C.* p. 134.

34. *N.D.C.* p. 105.

35. "The Frontiers of Criticism," *O.P.P.* p. 106.

36. "The Metaphysical Poets," *S.E.* p. 290.

37. "What is a Classic?" *O.P.P.* p. 53; cp. however "The Modern Mind," *U.P.U.C.* p. 129.

38. "What is a Classic?" *O.P.P.* p. 64.

39. "What is Minor Poetry?" *O.P.P.* p. 47; "Andrew Marvell," *S.E.* p. 292.

40. "Introduction," *S.W.*

41. Cp. "Thoughts After Lambeth," *S.E.* p. 368.

42. *A.S.G.* p. 25.

CHAPTER III

DIALECT OF THE TRIBE

We now come to Eliot's criticism properly speaking. So many critical theories claim to derive from Eliot that he seems rather in the position of the country squire in Smollett to whom young women in the neighbourhood ascribed their fatherless offspring, confident of his good-natured support. Such late essays as "The Frontiers of Criticism" record some bewilderment at this impossibly fertile paternity. His criticism, like his social polemic, is based on the two levels of "personality," the egocentric and the cultivated. Anyone who thinks of writing poetry as a self-expressive activity may imagine that he is creating something out of nothing, like God: but nothing like this happens. The impulse to write can only come from previous literary experience, and is conditioned by poetic conventions throughout. The new poem, like the new baby, is born into a verbal society, an order of words already there. Hence the view that "originality" consists in making a fresh start in literature is a half-truth. An essential part of creative power is in past literature. Every poet inherits a literary continuum which has come down from Homer to our own day, and feels that this continuum "has a simultaneous existence and composes a simultaneous order."[1] His relation to literary tradition may be implicit or explicit: the quotation and allusion so abundant in Eliot belong to the explicit relation. Education in the humanities ought to put us in possession of the common cultural tradition on which new poetry is based. Otherwise poetry will fail to communicate, and it is no good blaming the poet if it does.

Imitativeness is usually, and rightly, taken as a sign of immaturity in a poet. But when a poet achieves his own style, his relation to former poets becomes much more specific. "One of the surest of tests is the way in which a poet borrows. Immature poets imitate; mature poets steal."[2] Eliot is one of the poets who make a possessive use of sources. It is fascinating to compare a passage in A. C. Benson's *Life of Fitzgerald* with the opening lines of "Gerontion," or a passage in Charles Maurras with "Triumphal March," and see how Eliot divined the poetic possibilities inherent in these passages. There are also many altered or adapted lines: thus Chapman's "Under the chariot of the snowy Bear," itself an echo from Seneca, becomes "Beyond the circuit of the shuddering Bear" in "Gerontion." A very minor poem, the third of the "Five-Finger Exercises," is said to contain echoes from five poets in its fourteen lines.[3] Sometimes the echo is not verbal but structural, like the echo of Donne's "*Per fretum febris*, by these straits to die," at the end of "Gerontion." The faint aroma of Kipling's *They* around the rose-garden episode of "Burnt Norton" is more elusive, as is the "shadow" of Dowson's *Cynara* which is said to have influenced the shadow in *The Hollow Men*, a poem it could hardly resemble less. Of course we should not invariably assume that such allusions throw light on the meaning of the poem that echoes them, still less that the emotional effect of the original can simply be added to Eliot's poem by such an echo.

Eliot has also spoken of the importance of studying other languages than one's own. The poet should be a Burbank with a Baedeker, cross-breeding English with Continental and Classical traditions, as Eliot's study of Dante and of French *symbolisme* did for modern English poetry. The majority of Eliot's adaptations, however, are from English literature, and in any case the cross-breeding rule applies to phraseology rather than rhythm. The use of Dante's idiom in the second section of "Little

Gidding" is a *tour de force* unparalleled in English poetry, but it does not use the *terza rima* form. And in *Murder in the Cathedral* the reader must decide for himself whether the hymn "Still the horror" is closer in rhythm to *Dies Irae*, which is its model, or to *Hiawatha*.

We notice that allusive and echoic poetry often has a curiously penetrating quality about it. For Eliot the capacity of poetry to be unconsciously memorised is a criterion of genuineness, and the capacity of Eliot's own poetry for this is extraordinary. It is one thing to dislike his poetry or decry its reputation; it is another thing to forget it, once carefully read. His prodigious influence may even exaggerate his merits, for, as he says, "when we come to the point of making a statement about poetry, it is the poetry that sticks in our minds that weights that statement,"[4] and Eliot does stick in our minds. Perhaps the echoic aspect of his poetry gives us a minor clue to its mnemonic adhesiveness.

A certain amount of borrowing must be voluntary: but the main creative process is involuntary, or at least applied to something that does not depend on the will, like landing a fish. The poet has no idea of what he wants to say until he has found the words of his poem, and "When you have the words for it, the 'thing' for which the words had to be found has disappeared, replaced by a poem."[5] What the poet has at first is a kind of rhythm or movement, which becomes manifest in words and "may bring to birth the idea and the image."[6] The poet has experiences of no discernible pattern which may range from the smell of cooking to the reading of Spinoza; but in him they sink to the bottom of the mind, to "suffer a sea change" there—for Ariel's song seems to have some association in Eliot's mind with the process.[7] They then return as an amorphous something demanding verbal form. The poet may not know what is coming up, but whatever it is, his whole being is directed to realising it. One can see here another reason why humility is a major virtue to Eliot. The self-important ego has no place here: the poet, as Remy de Gourmont says, has to transmute his own personality drop by drop into the creative personality. The language of the poets who succeed in doing this shows a peculiar transparency. "Language in a healthy state presents the object, is so close to the object that the two are identified."[8]

When the amorphous thing appears clearly, it needs a name. Eliot calls it "emotion," a word which is not consistently distinguished from "feeling." It is not what we usually mean by emotion, however: it is a presentation, as immediate experience, of a complex of images and ideas. As Ezra Pound says, poetry provides equations, like mathematics, but equations for emotions. The capacity of the poet to produce such equations and of the reader to respond to them Eliot calls "sensibility." This is one of Eliot's favourite words, partly a translation of the French *sensibilité*, and it implies subtlety, delicacy and refinement. In practice, if not in theory, it seems to stop short of the quality that Eliot speaks of, in connexion with Shakespeare, as a "terrifying clairvoyance." The human clairvoyance of Shakespeare, the physical clairvoyance of Homer, the spiritual clairvoyance of Blake, seem to elude Eliot's sensibility, which turns rather to Dante, to Virgil, and to Baudelaire.

When the right words are there, the images and ideas of which they are now the transparent medium form what Eliot calls the "objective correlatives"[9] of the emotion. They make the emotion communicable to the reader, and are evidence that the poet's sensibility has been clarified. In great poetry we are aware of the variety of experiences that can be fused together, and great poetry differs from lesser poetry not by any ethical quality like "sublimity," but by an intensity of combination. Such poetry "fuses the old and obliterated and the trite, the current, and the new and surprising, the most ancient and the most civilised mentality."[10] In such unity of varieties there is "a recognition, implicit in the expression of every experience, of other kinds of experience which are possible."[11] Eliot has his "touchstone" passages: one is a speech in the third act of Tourneur's *Revenger's Tragedy*, and another is the final canto of the *Paradiso*. Of a passage in this canto Eliot says: "It is the real right thing, the power of establishing relations between beauty of the most diverse sorts; it is the utmost power of the poet."

Poets on the highest level possess, Eliot says, "a mechanism of sensibility which could devour any kind of experience."[12] The two aspects of this mechanism, subjective and objective, are often described by Eliot in terms of music and the visual arts respectively. Poetry begins in a rhythm too far down in the unconscious to be reached by the ego, and probably released by a relaxing of the normal inhibitions of consciousness. The awareness of this rhythm is an "auditory imagination," beautifully described by Eliot as "the feeling for syllable and rhythm, penetrating far below the conscious levels of thought and feeling, invigorating every word; sinking to the most primitive and forgotten, returning to the origin and bringing something back, seeking the beginning and the end."[13] The poet is concerned not to *say* anything, but to articulate this rhythm, and in this he resembles the composer; for the poetic "structure will first appear in terms of something analogous to musical form."[14] But the articulation itself takes the form of "clear visual images," which form the golden mean between "the extremes of incantation and meaning."[15] Images include concepts, for to the poet the concept is "a direct sensuous apprehension of thought, or a recreation of thought into feeling."[16]

In the age of Donne what Eliot calls sensibility was called wit, and what he calls an objective correlative was called a conceit, or something conceived. "Wit" has a more intellectual sound than "sensibility" or "emotion," and indicates why poetry of Donne's school is called "metaphysical." Its "metaphysical" quality is actually a technique of fusing images and ideas which is deliberately strained and forced. Hence there is a latent irony in its conceits, a suggestion of the grotesque which seems conscious, and so intellectual. The metaphysical poets had a unified sensibility, but their strained ingenuity shows the difficulty of retaining it at that time, with Milton and Puritanism around the corner. There is a similar feeling of explicit tension about unified sensibility when it revives in modern times with Laforgue and other *symbolistes*. The inference is that "it appears likely that poets in our civilization, as it exists at present, must be *difficult*."

Inferior poetry also has a subjective and an objective aspect, but of a different kind. Even the greatest poet may fail to perfect his work if the emotion gets wrapped around something in his personal life, and produces a spilled-over intensity not properly expressed in the poem. Eliot believes this to have happened with *Hamlet*. But inferior poetry falls into two types: poetry which is not objectively clarified, and remains emotionally murky, and poetry not conceived at the deepest level, and so written consciously and voluntarily. Eliot says these types constitute a "dissociation of sensibility," going to one or the other extreme of incantation and meaning.

We may meet a passage like this in Eliot's plays:

He has a heart of gold. But, not to beat about the bush,
He's rather a rough diamond.

The question whether this is "good poetry" or not depends simply on its appropriateness to the character of the person who speaks it. Such appropriateness is dramatic rhetoric in its proper sense of decorum. But a more egocentric craftsman might be unwilling to put a character into one of his plays who would naturally express himself in amiable clichés, as Eliot's Eggerson does here. If we read Seneca's plays, we notice a quality in them that we call rhetorical in a different sense, meaning that each speaker in turn is impressing us with his, or rather the author's, eloquence. The poetry has become verbal, in the sense that it is now an art of words, not an art of which words are the transparent medium. Seneca was a Stoic, and perhaps the rhetoric in his plays has something to do with Stoic spiritual pride. Such pride corresponded to strong tendencies in Elizabethan drama, reflected, if transcended, even by Shakespeare. Eliot's essay on Massinger is a particularly subtle analysis of this kind of rhetorical haze settling into a later writer.

Milton, for Eliot, is a more extreme example of an impressive rhetoric setting up a half-translucent curtain of sound in front of the visions. With the Romantics we find a cult of the oracular, a sense of the strangeness in reality which is perverted into "a short cut to the strangeness without the reality."[17] Here vagueness is felt to be a virtue. In Swinburne's soft-focus technique we feel that it is "the word that gives him the thrill, not the object." Such poetry tends to create a self-sufficient world of words, which does not even "depend upon some world which it simulates." Mallarmé among the *symbolistes*, and still more Maeterlinck, were affected by similar influences.

A simpler form of dissociation occurs when a poet is trying to evoke a mood by verbal magic. Such poetry seeks, not unity, but uniformity: it aims at its mood and excludes everything that might "disturb" it or break its spell. If the poem is intended to be serious, it is uniformly serious, that is, solemn. In Gray's *Elegy*, a poem for which Eliot has an unusually strong dislike, we settle into a country churchyard at night and have the appropriate feelings and reflexions, but there are no suggestions of other moods mixing with them, as there would be in Marvell; hence the feeling is cruder than in Marvell. This kind of dissociation seeks the sentimental, the ready-made associative path, and eventually collapses into an insipid sense of propriety. It is outraged when it finds such a line as "I shall wear the bottoms of my trousers rolled" in a poem that also mentions mermaids.

We can also have intellectual dissociation, where poetry does not transform its ideas into immediate emotional experience. Allegory in Dante is a method that "makes for simplicity and intelligibility," because "for a competent poet, allegory means *clear visual images*." A poet who fails to transmute concepts into direct apprehension is not so much intellectual as reflective or ruminating, as Eliot says of the later work of Tennyson and Browning, achieving the facile continuity of pursuing a train of thought. Actually meaning is subordinate to structure, and poets may "find it expedient to occupy their conscious mind with the craftsman's problems, leaving the deeper meaning to emerge from a lower level."[18] A poem may make its impact on a reader before the reader has started to think about what it means: the impact can be so disturbing that the meaning may even have a reassuring and sedative effect, keeping the reader's mind diverted and quiet, like a bit of meat thrown to a watchdog by a burglar.[19]

The conception of "clear visual images" as the mean between the extremes of incantation and meaning belongs, we should note, to the polemic of the nineteen-twenties rather than to literary criticism. Here as everywhere the road of excess leads to the palace of wisdom. Eliot has achieved his hold on the modern reader's imagination not by clear visual images, but by uniting the extremes of incantation and meaning:

> Dawn points, and another day
> Prepares for heat and silence. Out at sea the dawn wind
> Wrinkles and slides. I am here
> Or there, or elsewhere. In my beginning.

There is no doubt about the power of incantation in this passage, nor about the fact that, as Browning's Lippo says of the world, it means intensely, and means good. But it is not a poetry of clear visual images, the only word that even looks like one, "wrinkles," being an echo from Tennyson.

The poet's experiences are shaped into a unity which takes its place in a literary tradition. One would suppose that the shaping process has something to do with the literary tradition itself. How otherwise could the process be called, even as a figure of speech, impersonal? But I can find no proof-text in Eliot that clearly suggests how the literary tradition is embodied in conventions, genres and mythical structures, and how those in turn exert a defining power on the poet's mind. He says that there are two levels of impersonality, one the craftsman's level of convention, such as we have in an anthology piece of Lovelace or Campion, and a higher one "achieved by the maturing artist."[20] But convention does not conceal personality: it detaches and releases the poetic personality from the ordinary one. At the same time the word "impersonal," though perhaps deliberately paradoxical, does express part of our response to the greatest art, the feeling Eliot describes as "this realizes the genius of the language," as distinct from the feeling "this is a man of genius using the language."[21]

Eliot says that there are four ways of thinking: talking to others, to one other, to oneself, and to God—the identity of thinking and talking here is interesting—also that there are three voices of poetry, the poet talking to himself, to others, and through a character.[22] We may reduce these to two kinds of writing. Sometimes the poet is writing out what takes shape in his mind, and cannot think of an audience until he has finished. There are other genres which are inherently rhetorical, where the poet is conditioned by an audience during the act of writing. Of these, the one relevant to Eliot is poetic drama.

During the nineteen-twenties and nineteen-thirties

Eliot's popular reputation was that of an erudite high-brow of whom it was only to be expected that he should conclude his longest poem with a barrage of Sanskrit. But such a reputation would be contradictory to Eliot's view of the "élite" as responsible for articulating the un-conscious culture of their societies. Eliot would like, he says, an audience that could neither read nor write[23]—though one fears that this remark is based only on the cliché about the superiority of the uneducated to the half-educated. His criticism has always shown a pre-occupation with the possibility of verse drama, which, he says, no fatalistic philosophy of history should prevent us from trying to get.[24] The central problems of poetic drama, for him, have always been connected with versification and diction.

In self-expressive writing, something voluntary has buried itself into the act of writing. What results is often "free" verse in the sense of verse allowing an uninhibited flow from the expressing ego. No verse is free, Eliot says, for the man who wants to do a good job.[25] When bad free verse rhymes and scans, we call it doggerel. Eliot does not speak of doggerel, but he does employ a distinc-tion between "poetry" and "verse," leaving it, as here, in inverted commas. By "verse" is meant a kind of poetry which directly faces an audience, and is conditioned in expression by that audience. Eliot is fascinated by the problem of "verse," and recognises that some impor-tant poets, notably Kipling, are primarily writers of "verse."

The broadest form of "verse" is deliberate doggerel, which is used in *Sweeney Agonistes*, and closely related is "light verse," as we have it in *Old Possum's Book of Practical Cats*. One feels that the poems in strict quatrains, such as "The Hippopotamus," are closer to "verse" than "Gerontion" because more predictable in metre and more explicitly satiric in tone. The arranging of words in formal patterns gives an effect of conscious wit, and the use of long words like "Polyphiloprogenitive" is broadly comic. Yet even in "Prufrock" the tumbling down of wistful reverie into preoccupation is represented by an artful sinking from "poetry" into "verse":

Should I, after tea and cakes and ices,
Have the strength to force the moment to its crisis?

Finally, there is the continuous poem addressed to a listening audience, which, whether epic or narrative or drama, needs a predictable metre and consequently some basis in "verse."

The effect of "verse" is normally continuous, and once a regular rhythm is set up, a habitual or expected quality enters the writing. The effect of "poetry" is rather to arrest the movement and force the reader's mind to intensify instead of going forward. "Poetry" thus seems to be essentially discontinuous. One of the most obvious features of *The Waste Land* and *Four Quartets* is the fact that they are written in a discontinuous sequence of movements: the continuity of the poems as a whole has been, so to speak, handed over to the reader. But in verse drama the problem of continuity can no longer be avoided or solved in this way. "No poet can write a poem of amplitude," Eliot says, "unless he is a master of the prosaic,"[26] and again, "the poet who could not write 'verse' when verse was needed, would be without that sense of structure which is required to make a poem of any length readable."[27] In Shakespeare the moments of greatest poetic intensity, such as Macbeth's "To-morrow" speech, are also the moments of greatest dramatic intensity. In drama, then, two principles are involved: a structural principle, concerned with the total design, of which the basis is "verse," and a textural principle, which moves from "verse" into "poetry" in moments of intensity, and back into "verse" in moments of relaxation, where continuity of structure is the important thing.

What holds these together is a "common style," which is produced by a "collaboration between a great many people talking a living language and a very few people writing it."[28] This style is conversational, not the grand style of rhetoric, where there is a standard to be met, and so a sense of "sinking" whenever the rhetoric relaxes. Dante is the greatest master of such common style, and hence the best model for imitation. Shakespeare, with his dazzling verbal cleverness, departs more from common style, and Milton abandons it. But to get out of touch with common style is literary decadence, and the balance must right itself. There have been three main revolutions of diction in English literature attempting to rescue the common style. The first was that of Waller and Denham, completed by Dryden, against Miltonic Baroque; the second was that of Wordsworth; the third was that of Eliot and Pound against the dissociated Georgians.[29]

"Verse" normally has, first, a metrical pattern, such as the iambic pentameter of Shakespeare. Second, it has a prose or semantic rhythm which is simultaneously present and syncopates against it. There is, third, in English verse, an accentual stress-pattern, which in iambic pentameter usually has four beats. This four-stress line is the bedrock of English versification: it is the rhythm of alliterative verse, of nursery rhymes and of ballads, all rhythms close to Eliot. It differs from a metre in being a musical rhythm, in which the number of syllables between stresses is variable. In Eliot this rhythm is heard most clearly in *Sweeney Agonistes*, where the variable number of syllables syncopates against a heavy beat, producing a verbal parallel to jazz. Such a stress-pattern is useful only for parody. In the plays we have an accentual line, close to prose in effect, which Eliot describes as a line of three main beats with a caesura.[30] Naturally he must know, but this is my book, and what I hear is four beats:

Well, not directly. *J*ulia had a *te*legram
*Ask*ing her to *come*, and to *bring* me *with* her.
*J*ulia was de*layed*, and *sent* me on a*head*.

Such lines are quite different in effect from the opening
lines of "Prufrock," where the pattern of three beats and a
caesura is much easier to see, and even more different from
the short lines in which the Quartets (except "East Coker")
end, and which are three-beat lines without caesura.

In the early poetry we often find a rhythm very like
that of Jacobean drama, except that the accentual
pattern has come to dominate the metrical one. In the
last part of "Gerontion" the long final words ("adul-
terated," "deliberations," "inquisition") fit into a four-
stress conception of the line much more neatly than into
pentameter. Elsewhere the accentual rhythm is varied in
a great number of ways. Let us look at the famous opening lines of *The Waste Land*:

> April is the cruelest month, breeding
> Lilacs out of the dead land, mixing
> Memory and desire, stirring
> Dull roots with spring rain.

The first line, which establishes the tonality, is a normal
four-stress line. In the second the second stress hovers
over unaccented beats and comes down on a syncopated
one. In the third line the third stress is a "rest," occurring
in the pause between "desire" and "stirring." The fourth
line is really a two-stress line in which each stress has
been split in two by falling on a spondee, and so assimi-
lated to the four-stress pattern. We can sometimes see a
connexion with some of the earlier four-stress patterns in
English prosody, such as medieval alliterative verse:
compare the rhythm of

> Ganga was sunken, and the limp leaves
> Waited for rain, while the black clouds . . .

with this from *Sir Gawain and the Green Knight*:

> The brygge was brayde doun, and the brode gates
> Unbarred and born open upon bothe halve. . . .

Each of the short sections of the longer poems has as a rule its own rhythmical pattern. The third section of "East Coker" begins with a rhythm based on a six-stress line, heard very clearly in "Dis*ting*uished *ci*vil *ser*vants, *chair*men of *ma*ny com*mit*tees." The line "And *cold* the *sense* and *lost* the *mo*tive of *ac*tion" has five stresses, but we feel that the first two occupy the time of three. *Murder in the Cathedral* has passages of five-stress lines, which, being longer than pentameters, can accommodate more easily the polysyllabic clatter of modern educated speech:

> I see nothing quite conclusive in the art of
>   temporal government,
> But violence, duplicity and frequent malversation.

Such a line is cumbersome for ordinary dialogue, though it fits the specialised hieratic context it was designed for well enough.

In the early poems no reader can miss the rhetorical contrast between the sharp realism, full of dingy words and calculated bathos, and the dreamy romanticism, full of "dying falls," which distinguish the world of crumpets from the world of trumpets, in the words of "A Cooking Egg." In his essay on Dante Eliot distinguishes the "low dream," the wish-fulfilment of the ego, from the "high dream" or vision which is Dante's proper subject. In the devotional poetry we have again two contrasting styles, that of the "high dream," and deliberately prosaic passages indicating a return to ordinary consciousness. The rhetoric of the "high dream" does not differ greatly from that of the "low dream" in the early poems except in being free from parody and in a few special features. One of these is a technique of repetition of sound representing a concentration on a single idea. The opening of the fifth section of *Ash Wednesday*, with such lines as "Against the Word the unstilled world still whirled," is an example. A practice of inter-rhyming ("Words, after speech, reach"; "It tosses up our losses," etc.) has something of the same rhetorical function.

The transition from "poetry" to "verse" in the dramas may be measured by the role of the chorus in them. Rymer, the denigrator of *Othello*, once remarked: "What Reformation may not we expect, now that in France they see the necessity of a Chorus to their Tragedies?" and Eliot also begins full of enthusiasm for the chorus. *Sweeney Agonistes* is really a continuous chorus, and the choruses in *The Rock* are the only valuable part of the play, or pageant. In *Murder in the Cathedral* the chorus has its traditional role of providing an emotional tension alternating with that of the action. In *The Family Reunion* the minor characters occasionally form a chorus, and the more articulate ones sometimes withdraw from dialogue into monologue. Eliot has criticised these passages as too much like operatic arias, but surely every speech that does not directly advance the action *is* an operatic aria. In any case the chorus in *The Cocktail Party* is cut down to one scene, and in the next two plays it disappears altogether.

Thus the plays show a gradual retreat from "poetry" into "verse" which tightens up the structure, perhaps at the cost of other qualities. Eliot is well aware of the importance of structure in drama as being what Aristotle called its "soul," the integrity whereby a "reality of moral synthesis"[31] is conveyed. Many readers of Eliot feel that no character in the plays matches in vividness the characterisation of Prufrock or Gerontion or Sweeney. Eliot speaks of the way in which "the creation of a character in a drama consists in the process of transfusion of the personality, or, in a deeper sense, the life, of the author into the character."[32] But for Eliot himself "poetry" is clearly essential to this full transmutation, and there seems to be something in the plays and their "verse" which tends to inhibit its fullness.

The two *genres* of Eliot's work, drama, and the kind of non-dramatic poem which is, as he says, a form of "meditative verse" and not a lyric, sum up between them the public and the private aspects of literature. The basis of the former is "verse," of the latter, "poetry." When Eliot speaks of poetic drama, he seems to think of it as an ideal combination of public and private utterance. He describes this ideal genre eloquently, in language anticipating *Four Quartets*, when he says that at a play we may "perceive a pattern behind the pattern into which the characters deliberately involve themselves; the kind of pattern which we perceive in our own lives only at rare moments of inattention and detachment, drowsing in sunlight."[33] We may feel that no drama of Eliot quite reaches this ideal. But then Eliot assumes that poetic drama is always and necessarily a stage play. This assumption is consistent with his view of the stratification of culture, but even so it may be questioned. Perhaps *The Waste Land*, where loveliness peeps fitfully through squalor and an invisible divine presence haunts the misery of Europe, is closer to what Eliot really means by poetic drama than any of his plays.

Drama, an ensemble performance for an audience, is the most striking example of the fact that the arts belong to the continuum of tradition and culture, and form part of its civilising influence. In great drama there is something for all levels of society at once.[34] But although the life of civilised man is superior to the barbarian, there is still the third level of which culture is a continuous imitation, the level of religion.

Acceptance of a specific tradition is not uncritical relativism, doing in Rome as the Romans do merely because they do it. There are wider laws of reason and beauty that make all human culture intelligible to every culture. This is so obvious that many feel that we should obliterate our local cultures and merge them into a global uniformity. Eliot does not share this view, but he recognises, in changing his mind about Goethe, the link between catholicity of taste and universality of outlook—in this case "the problem of reconciliation and the definition of the Great European." In the same essay he remarks that "wisdom is *logos κοινός*, the same for all men everywhere." This phrase ("common logos") comes from an aphorism of Heraclitus, for whom logos meant much more than simply word or reason, because "to the Greek there was something inexplicable about logos so that it was a participation of man in the divine."[35] This aphorism is one of the two mottoes of *Four Quartets*.

We need, to begin with, some sense of reality which absorbs the ego into society. This means a set of specific loyalties, to a family, to a local culture, to a church, at most to a nation. In these loyalties our sense of individuality is not lost but fulfilled. Still, we cannot find ultimate reality in them: we are driven towards something universal, the same for all men everywhere. If we try to expand our loyalties, replacing a people with Mankind, a church with Truth or Goodness, something goes wrong. We lose our original sense of individuality as our loyalties get broader and fuzzier. Speaking of Stoical and other philosophies, Eliot says: "A man does not join himself with the Universe so long as he has anything else to join himself with."[36] The universal we reach ought to include within it the individuality with which we started: it should be a supreme Self which gives each self its identity.

The ego lives in a world of illusion in which the primary categories are those of time and space. Time as we ordinarily experience it has three dimensions, past, present and future. None of these dimensions exists: the past is no longer, the future not yet, the present never quite. The centre of time is now, but there is no such time as now. Similarly, the centre of space is "here," but there is no such place as here. All places are "there": the best we can do is to draw a circle around ourselves and say that here is inside it. The result of the egocentric view is loneliness, a sense of alienation from a world that keeps running away from it.

For man in his social context, time and space have more meaning. Tradition gives meaning to time, and a localised culture surrounds a part of nature and makes it "here." But the historical perspective can breed new fallacies, such as the genetic fallacy, the tendency to disown the past by assuming that religion and culture are essentially what they have developed from, instead of "accustoming ourselves to find meaning in *final causes* rather than in origins."[37] No structure of reason or science founded on the illusions of ordinary perception can remove its own foundations: what is needed is a transformation of ordinary perception itself, some kind of direct experience that is individual but not egocentric, in contact with reality and not with appearance.

This line of thought naturally leads to an interest in the mystics. For the mystic, ordinary experience is attained by ordinary consciousness: if we feel that such experience is not real enough, we must turn to real consciousness, ordinary experience on a higher plane. Such a consciousness, curiously enough, brings us to more primitive and archaic modes of thought, especially in conceiving time and space. The appearance of time, the past-present-future continuum, belongs to a world of becoming, where there is no identity because everything changes into something else. Over against it is a world which is not timeless, but a world where "all is always now." Similarly the illusion of space, the length-breadth-thickness continuum of "there," becomes "here," the area covered by a focus of consciousness. The mystic finds, at the heart of the illusion of time, a real present, and, at the heart of the illusion of space, a real presence.

Eliot's first philosophical interest was in F. H. Bradley. In Bradley's *Appearance and Reality*, "appearance" is a mass of logically impossible and self-contradictory impressions of time, space, change, causation and the like, where there is a huge fission between subject and object, "mine" and "this." We have to go on to a reality which is an "Absolute," where all contradictions of appearance are reconciled. The Absolute can only be reached by an "immediate experience" in which reason, will and feeling all fulfil themselves. Thus what started as a nineteenth-century idealist's problem about how far we can "know reality" ends as a kind of mystical primer. In the Indian philosophy which Eliot next studied, the ego is a product of an automatic natural energy, called *karma*, which expresses itself as desire, and involves one in suffering. Over against this is a consciousness of a self beyond mind and body, a self which is not a separate ego but identical with a total self (Atman). The end of the process, summed up in the phrase "Thou art That," is an objectivity which achieves self-identification, a paradoxical union very like that of the poetic process in Eliot.

In Christianity, logos means, not word, reason, or universal wisdom, but the Person of Christ. This Logos enters the continuum of history at a point in time and stays there, and ever since each moment is a potential moment of real as well as of ordinary consciousness. Our progress toward real consciousness may take us in either of two opposite directions, which reach the same point. "The way up and the way down are one and the same," Heraclitus says, in an aphorism which is the second motto of the Quartets. We may call these ways the way of plenitude and the way of vacancy, to use terms found in "Burnt Norton." The former is exemplified by the encyclopaedic symbolism of Dante's *Commedia*; the other is described by St John of the Cross as a "dark night of the soul," where by an ascesis of everything that attaches us outwardly, we reach the same divine presence.

Poetry is also a direct and total experience, "the experience both of a moment and of a lifetime." It carries us beyond ordinary consciousness because it is "a function of all art to give us some perception of an order in life, by imposing an order upon it." We listen to a symphony in ordinary time, but its beginning implies an end; we look at a picture in ordinary space, but its tense energy is arrested movement, as a Chinese jar gives us a sense that it "Moves perpetually in its stillness." Thus art is a technique of meditation, using that word in its technical sense as a means of learning to experience reality. The complete absorption in the object demanded of the poet recurs in the religious life: in comparing Donne's sermons with Andrewes', for example, Eliot says that Donne "is constantly finding an object which shall be adequate to his feelings; Andrewes is wholly absorbed in the object and therefore responds with the adequate emotion." Art is a psychopomp only, however, or, as Eliot says in a passage clearly intended to be a central statement of his belief: "It is ultimately the function of art, in imposing a credible order upon reality, and thereby eliciting some perception of an order *in* reality, to bring us to a condition of serenity, stillness, and reconciliation; and then leave us, as Virgil left Dante, to proceed toward a region where that guide can avail us no farther."[38] The serenity and stillness at the end of the *Purgatorio* or Shakespeare's romances is itself an experience, and a very profound one: but it is also a condition of a further kind of experience of which poetry is the shadow and not the substance.

It is obvious that the quality of poetry is not affected by the poet's beliefs; nor does the poet *qua* poet believe at all: it is what he produces, not what he believes, that is his poetry, even if he could not have produced it without belief. There are many discussions of this point in Eliot, some of them very inconclusive. In general, however, what he finds in Christianity does not give him a formula for value-judgments on poetry, but a conception of the function and context of poetry. We start with what he calls, quoting Andrewes, "The word within the word, unable to speak a word," at the hidden centre of reality.

And, for Eliot as for Coleridge before him, we end with the Word as the circumference of reality, containing within itself time, space, and poetry viewed in the light of "the conception of poetry as a living whole of all the poetry that has ever been written."[39] This last is an experience of poetry as the Song of Man which is also, like the poem which inspired St John of the Cross, the Song of Songs, and also, like the *Bhagavadgita*, to Eliot the greatest poem in the world next to Dante, the Song of God.

REFERENCES

1. "Tradition and the Individual Talent," *S.E.* p. 14.

2. "Philip Massinger," *S.E.* p. 206.

3. Smith, p. 254 (the fullest treatment of Eliot's sources).

4. "Matthew Arnold,'' *U.P.U.C.* p. 113.

5. "The Three Voices of Poetry," *O.P.P.* pp. 97–98.

6. "The Music of Poetry," *O.P.P.* p. 38.

7. "Conclusion," *U.P.U.C.* p. 146.

8. "Swinburne as Poet," *S.E.* p. 327.

9. This famous phrase occurs in "Hamlet," *S.E.* p. 145.

10. "Matthew Arnold," *U.P.U.C.* p. 119.

11. "Andrew Marvell," *S.E.* p. 303; cp. preface to Valéry, *Art of Poetry*, tr. Folliot, (1958), xxiii.

12. "The Metaphysical Poets," *S.E.* p. 287.

13. "Matthew Arnold," *U.P.U.C.* pp. 118–19.

14. "Rudyard Kipling," *O.P.P.* p. 238.

15. "Johnson as Critic and Poet," *O.P.P.* p. 169.

16. "The Metaphysical Poets," *S.E.* pp. 286, 288, 298.

17. "Imperfect Critics," *S.W.*

18. "Rudyard Kipling," *O.P.P.* p. 238.

19. "Conclusion," *U.P.U.C.* p. 151.

20. "Yeats," *O.P.P.* p. 255.

21. "What is a Classic?" *O.P.P.* p. 63.

22. "Charles Whibley," *S.E.* p. 501; cp. *O.P.P.* p. 87.

23. "Conclusion," *U.P.U.C.* p. 152.

24. "A Dialogue on Dramatic Poetry," *S.E.* p. 56.

25. Cp. "The Music of Poetry," *O.P.P.* p. 37.

26. *Op. cit.*, 32.

27. "Rudyard Kipling," *O.P.P.* p. 251.

28. "Byron," *O.P.P.* p. 201.

29. "The Music of Poetry," *O.P.P.* p. 31.

30. "Poetry and Drama," *O.P.P.* p. 82; cp. Gardner, p. 46 ff.

31. "Thomas Heywood," *S.E.* p. 175.

32. "Ben Jonson," *S.E.* p. 157.

33. "John Marston," *S.E.* p. 232.

34. "Conclusion," *U.P.U.C.* p. 153.

35. "Second Thoughts about Humanism," *S.E.* p. 485n.

36. "Shakespeare and the Stoicism of Seneca," *S.E.* p. 131.

37. "Dante," *S.E.* p. 250.

38. "Poetry and Drama," *O.P.P.* p. 87.

39. "Tradition and the Individual Talent," *S.E.* p. 17.

CHAPTER IV

UNREAL CITY

Eliot's earlier poetry is mainly satiric, and presents a world that may be summed up as a world without laughter, love or children. The laughter is of the sinister and terrible kind that psychologists say the laughter in dreams is: we have the laughing woman in "Hysteria," Sweeney "Letting his arms hang down to laugh," and Mr Apollinax laughing "like an irresponsible foetus." The few children are shadowy, sinister or pathetic, like the blank-faced urchin in "Rhapsody on a Windy Night" and the ragged girl who watches the pompous Directeur "Et crève d'amour"—this being the only use of the word "love," I think, in Eliot's poetry before *Ash Wednesday*. After *The Hollow Men* the poetry becomes increasingly devotional in tone, but there is no real change of attitude, only a back and a front view from the same poetic edifice. In the later poetry the "I," the speaker of the poem, is a *persona* of the poet himself; in the earlier work the narrators are created characters, speaking with the poet's voice but not for him.

A curious, and to me regrettable, feature of Eliot's critical theory is his avoidance of the term "imagination," except in the phrase "auditory imagination" at the furthest remove from the poetic product. The poet has an image-forming power, and his "philosophy" or body of "ideas" is arrived at by studying the conceptual implications of the structure of his images. Thus Yeats writes an essay called "The Philosophy of Shelley's Poetry," which is actually an essay on Shelley's imagery. This seems to me a much more valid critical procedure than talking about the poetry and the ideas of a poet as though they were separable things, separable enough even for a poet to "borrow" his philosophy from somebody else. Eliot's myth of decline contrasts Dante, who "had behind him the system of St. Thomas, to which his poem corresponds point to point," with Blake and Goethe and Shelley, who mistakenly invented their own philosophies. Blake's genius required, we are told, "a framework of accepted and traditional ideas which would have prevented him from indulging in a philosophy of his own." But when we read *Four Quartets*, whatever influences there may be from Bradley or Patanjali or St John of the Cross or Heraclitus, we darkly suspect Eliot too of indulging in a philosophy of his own.

Eliot speaks of the "major" poet as one whose entire work has a unity which is greater than the sum of its parts.[1] Elsewhere he speaks of the "world" that a poet creates, and remarks that all Shakespeare's work is one poem.[2] Eliot is clearly a major poet in this sense: he cannot be sampled in anthologies, and we understand each poem of his better for having read the others. But, if we are right, his total work is an imaginative world, and must be approached through his imagery, as Yeats approached Shelley. Yeats says: "I only made my pleasure in (Shelley) contented pleasure by massing in my imagination his recurring images ... till his world had grown solid underfoot and consistent enough for the soul's habitation." Let us see if we can domesticate ourselves in Eliot's world in the same way.

Poets tend to identify, by metaphor, the different aspects of cyclical movement in nature. Winter, death or old age, night, ruins and the sea have ready-made associations with each other, and so have spring, youth or birth, dawn, the city, and rain or fountains. Eliot's fondness for cyclical imagery meets us at every turn. The December setting of *Murder in the Cathedral*, the cold March of *The Family Reunion*, the "midwinter spring" of

"Little Gidding," are deeply wrought into the texture of the imagery. In "The Dry Salvages" he says of the cycle of water:

> His rhythm was present in the nursery bedroom,
> In the rank ailanthus of the April dooryard,
> In the smell of grapes on the autumn table,
> And the evening circle in the winter gaslight.

In "Portrait of a Lady" there is a sequence of four encounters carefully dated December, April, August and October. The opening page of *The Waste Land* starts with April and goes through the coming of summer to the word "winter." The five little lyrics called "Landscapes" are arranged in the order of the seasons, and the sea-gull in the last poem has a special association with the end of the cycle, re-appearing in "Gerontion" and the fourth section of *The Waste Land*. These groups of images make up not only a cycle but an opposition. Youth and age, spring and winter, dawn and darkness, rain and sea, form two contrasting states. Blake calls these states innocence and experience, and his terms are useful even for Eliot. For poets with a religious imagination, there are also heaven and hell, the paradisal and demonic realities underlying the mixture of good and evil in human life. Heaven and hell can be represented in poetry only by images of existence, hence images of innocence, the garden, perpetual spring, eternal youth, are closely associated with heaven or paradise, and images of repugnant experience, the desert, the sea, the prison, the tomb, are associated with hell. But for any poet who follows this structure of symbolism, including Eliot, there are four worlds, and heaven and innocence, hell and experience, are distinguished as well as associated.

In Dante's *Commedia* we have a *Paradiso* and an *Inferno*, and two intermediate worlds on the surface of this earth. One is the world of experience, the Europe of 1300, which permeates the whole poem by allusion and illustration. The other is the mountain of the *Purgatorio*, where Dante journeys upward in quest of innocence and reaches the Garden of Eden. For Eliot, there would be two places in Dante's world charged with a peculiar intensity: the place where the vision of experience begins to be a vision of hell, and the place where the vision of innocence begins to be a vision of paradise.

The former place is described in Canto 3 of the *Inferno*, where Dante, guided by Virgil, passes through the gates of hell into a crowd of people who lived "without blame or praise." They are not strictly in hell, because they "never were alive," and can neither live nor die. "Let us not speak of them, but look and pass on," says Virgil, so Dante goes on to the brink of the river Acheron, on the opposite shore of which is hell proper, the frontier that Eliot sometimes speaks of as crossed by a soul when it commits a mortal sin.

This scene is closely associated in Eliot's mind with the vision of modern life in Baudelaire's *Fleurs du mal*, expecially in "Au lecteur" and the opening of "Les septs vieillards." In Baudelaire modern life in the "fourmillante cité" is characterised by boredom or ennui. Ennui is not so much sin as the state of sin: it is kept from positive vice, not by virtue, but by the negative vices of indolence and fear. For real vice "Notre âme, hélas! n'est pas assez hardie," Baudelaire says; one lives in a world that Ecclesiastes calls "vanity," or mist. The dedication of Eliot's Prufrock volume quotes a passage from the *Purgatorio* ending "Treating shadows as a solid thing," and the feeling that what the world calls substance is really shadow runs all through Eliot's poetry.

There are three ways of reacting to this world. One is to live in it without realising that one is really dead, a realisation that may take many years, as Mary says in *The Family Reunion*. Another is to recognise its unreality and scramble up into daylight, in other words to live an honest life that is at least not futile. A third is the full understanding that such a world is not only the entrance to hell, but that all hell is implicit in it. Eliot speaks of "the boredom, and the horror, and the glory,"[3] which describe three of his four worlds. His vision of evil, however, is seldom a vision of horror or violence, except off-stage, as in the crucifixion of Celia Coplestone in *The Cocktail Party*. There seem to be sinister goings-on in the background of "Sweeney Among the Nightingales," but all that we see clearly is a dull brothel with yawning whores and gaping pimps. The misery of war-torn Europe is in the background of *The Waste Land*, but all we hear are voices asking querulously, "Are you alive, or not?" We have to see in such incidents as the seduction of the typist, who lets her body be used like a public urinal because "she is bored and tired," the full horror of the denial of humanity.

The motto of "Prufrock" comes from later in the *Inferno*, but it echoes Virgil's remark in Canto 3 that "The world does not allow the report of (such people) to exist." Prufrock himself would like to be Lazarus, come back from the dead, but is out of touch with the power that could perform such a miracle. In *The Waste Land* the poet, watching the crowds on London Bridge, repeats another line from the same Canto 3: "I had not thought death had undone so many." Most of the people are coming out of tube-stations, and the subway is a good image for this waste-land world because, like Dante's scene, it is just below the surface of the ground. The third section of "Burnt Norton" takes us further into this "place of disaffection," a world neither of daylight nor darkness, inhabited by "unhealthy souls" who seem less souls than the bloodless shades of a Homeric Hades.

In *The Hollow Men* we are "Gathered on the beach of this tumid river," the Acheron-Thames, separated from the "lost violent" souls in the real hell, who apparently include the Kurtz of Conrad's *Heart of Darkness*. Kurtz had a sense not of the boredom but of "the horror," and he is really "dead," whereas the hollow men are merely not alive, and cannot make the act of surrender involved in actual death. Like others later in the *Inferno*, the hollow men respond passively to winds, "behaving as the wind behaves," a parody of the Holy Spirit blowing where it pleases. The wind suggests also Gerontion driven by the Trades, the crowds in "Burnt Norton" driven by wind or expelled from the tube-stations like an eructation, and the statement in *The Rock* that "Man without God is a seed upon the wind, driven this way and that." Images of blown seeds, of scarecrows or "old guys," of bubbles and vapors, of shadowy and fitful appearances like Hadrian's "animula, vagula, blandula," represent a conception of the soul far removed from the Christian spiritual body. In the plays, too, the action usually turns on the growing realisation of the emptiness of the dead-alive world by the central character, flanking whom are subordinate characters who get back into ordinary life.

The opposite pole, at which the vision of innocence becomes paradisal, meets us at the end of Canto 26 of the *Purgatorio*, where Dante purges himself of his last sin, lechery, and is about to enter the ring of fire that separates him from Eden. The closing lines of this canto, beginning with "Ara vos prec," the original title of Eliot's 1920 book of poems, are frequently alluded to in Eliot. The image of refining fire, especially as a cure for lechery, is the organising image of "The Fire Sermon" in *The Waste Land*, and similar imagery dominates "Little Gidding." In Eden, where Dante renews the innocence of childhood, or rather of the childhood of man, the state of Adam before his fall, he meets a young girl, Matilda, who is gathering flowers and is compared to Proserpine.

All through Eliot's work runs the image of a "secret garden" (a phrase in *The Confidential Clerk*), associated with childhood, with spring flowers and rains, with a young girl, and with innocence—or at least leaving it is associated with guilt. In "La Figlia che Piange," the narrator's memory revolves around a girl with "her arms full of flowers," deserted by a man "As the soul leaves the body torn and bruised." A similar Matilda figure appears in *The Waste Land* as the "hyacinth girl," where the narrator speaks of "Looking into the heart of light, the silence." The phrase "heart of light" recurs in the rose-garden episode at the beginning of "Burnt Norton." In *The Family Reunion* Harry tells Agatha of his childhood at Wishwood and of a "rose-garden" which one enters, like Alice in Wonderland, through a "little door."

This situation is parodied in other poems. In "Portrait of a Lady" the narrator, a most un-heroic character pre-occupied with "self-possession," goes through a series of interviews with an aging spinster surrounded with the atmosphere of blighted romance ("Juliet's tomb"). He finally drifts off leaving her "Slowly twisting the lilac stalks" and staring bleakly into the loneliness of what is left of her life. In "Dans le restaurant" an old waiter is reminded by spring rains of a sexual experience he had in childhood with a little girl. The narrator is disgusted by the teller of the story, but his attitude to the story itself is more ambivalent: "De quel droit payes-tu des expériences comme moi?" he says.

Prufrock and Gerontion are talking to themselves, and the "you" addressed in both poems is "a familiar compound ghost," made up chiefly of memories. But Prufrock's meditation is called a love song, and sometimes the "you" takes on a female aspect; in "Gerontion" the only connexion of the "you" with anything feminine is the fact that the main subject of the last paragraph is passion and the stimulation of the senses. But a vestigial Matilda figure is still there in both poems, and the fact that she is so shadowy is part of Prufrock's frustration and Gerontion's cynicism. In "A Cooking Egg," the narrator, taking off from Villon's complaint of having lived an inglorious life for thirty years, contrasts his earlier life with

Pipit, a "penny world" that was still a world of eagles and trumpets, with his desiccated adult life. The curious title means, apparently, a not-so-fresh egg: the egg as a symbol of a self-enclosed existence meets us again in *Sweeney Agonistes*. For a woman, a similar childhood memory would be of a boy, like that of Marie in *The Waste Land*, who remembers her quasi-sexual excitement in sledding with her cousin, and associates mountains with freedom thereafter. In Dante Matilda gives place to Beatrice, and Beatrice is the "high dream" inspired by a childhood memory—Dante says at the age of nine, which according to Eliot is probably too late.[4] Most of the above parodies are childhood memories on the ego-centric level of the "low dream."

The most concentrated of all visions of a lost or transitory state of innocence is the rose-garden episode in "Burnt Norton," where we enter "our first world," a world full of invisible presences, and where the water of life and the two traditional paradisal flowers, the lotus of the East and the rose of the West, appear briefly before the vision fades. The phrase "the leaves were full of children" suggests that the children are the tree they are in, the tree of life. Parental or guardian figures, "dignified, invisible," are also present; perhaps even a divine presence inhabits the garden, as was said of the original Eden. In ordinary life the rose-garden is usually some kind of private or hidden retreat: but all such retreats are screen memories of man's lost innocence. Since the fall, Eden has been closed up, guarded by angels. In "Mr. Eliot's Sunday Morning Service" we have a glimpse of a paradise "Sustained by staring Seraphim," but in the foreground we see only "sable presbyters" darkening the window-pane, merging into the "epicene" bees "Along the garden-wall." In "Triumphal March" the hero is still in contact with a paradisal vision, but the "hedge" that the soldiers of his preposterous retinue make around him indicates that he is unlikely to remain so.

We notice the prominence of the word "light" at the end of this poem. Eden now lies at the centre of human consciousness, too deep for even dreams to reach, as the "heart of light" shining in an uncomprehending darkness. Its threatening angels are usually replaced in Eliot by birds or animals. In "Gerontion" the tiger, a traditional symbol of Antichrist, is the symbol of wrath, the eternal spiritual opposition of the worlds of Christ and Gerontion. In "Burnt Norton" a thrush first leads us into and then drives us out of the rose-garden, and a raven appears in the corresponding section of *The Family Reunion*. The childish discovery of forbidden knowledge in "Dans le restaurant" is interrupted by a "gros chien," and a dog in *The Waste Land* is introduced as a "friend to men," who scratches up corpses and is consequently a nuisance to those who want to stay buried. The point of view of the latter is represented by a much less enterprising dog, the Yorkshire terrier of "Five-Finger Exercises," who remains "safe and warm" in the midst of a brown waste land with a dry tree.

The worlds of experience and innocence, the subway and the rose-garden, may be called respectively, using terms from *The Hollow Men*, "death's dream kingdom" and "death's other kingdom." The reader may have begun to suspect that they are the "objective correlatives" of the two levels of personality dealt with in the previous chapters. Death's dream kingdom is the world of Prufrock and Gerontion, the "cracked and brown" waste land, the stubble field of the hollow men. As it is a world without identity, it is a world of "deliberate disguises," usually symbolised in Eliot, following another hint from Baudelaire's "Au lecteur," as animals— a different use of the animal from the one just mentioned, though related. The narrator in "Portrait of a Lady" says:

> And I must borrow every changing shape
> To find expression . . . dance, dance

Like a dancing bear,
Cry like a parrot, chatter like an ape.

and the narrator in "Mélange adultère du tout"
proposes a series of camouflages, the climax a birthday in Africa when he will be "Vêtu d'une peau de
girafe."

Human consciousness cannot identify permanently
with innocence or with experience. If it could, they
would become the eternal realities of heaven or hell.
Those who accept experience voluntarily can only do so
through detachment, not through identification, still
less through the dead-alive indifference which in the
third section of "Little Gidding" is carefully distinguished from detachment. The chorus in *Murder in the
Cathedral* achieves a momentary identification with experience in the "death-bringers" chorus, which thereby
becomes an epiphany of hell; hence its imagery is full of
animals, leading to "the horror of the ape." In the rose-
garden episode of "Burnt Norton" innocence becomes,
for an instant, an epiphany of paradise. We notice that
Becket's comment on the chorus and the thrush's comment on the rose-garden vision are the same: "Human
kind cannot bear very much reality."

Death's other kingdom is, besides the vision of lost
innocence, the heaven of religion, appearing in this form
in *The Hollow Men* as the "multifoliate rose" of Dante's
Paradiso. Many do not believe in a future or eternal life,
but another aspect of death's other kingdom is irrefut-
able—the past. The great cultural achievements of the
past remain in the present to represent another world
which is both here and out of reach. Thus the wretched
couple in "Lune de miel," unable to sleep for bugs and
stench, are mocked by the Byzantine "forme précise"
of St Apollinaire, who, being stone, has no impulse to
scratch. We are always in a later phase of our cycle, individual or historical, than our past, and thus a sense of

losing energy or innocence is practically inseparable from consciousness itself.

The two kingdoms are also contrasted in the minds of Prufrock and Gerontion, who exemplify a theme, running through all of Eliot's work, of assuming a double part. In addressing a "you" who is also themselves, they follow a dialectic which separates the world they are in, and have committed themselves to, from a paradisal world set over against it, which they contemplate until they feel finally separated from it. In "Prufrock" this latter world is a wish-fulfilment world symbolised by the sea. It is the sea of the mermaids, as opposed to the sea of ordinary experience in which Prufrock awakens and "drowns," the latter being the sea in which he is a pair of ragged claws, and which in the apocalypse, according to the Bible, will disappear, taking Prufrock with it. Gerontion, as his name indicates, is an old man at the point of death, his reverie a parody of Newman's *The Dream of Gerontius*. All the images surrounding him are of the end of the natural cycle: the decaying house which is a symbol of his dying body, the gull, the sea, and the winter. Gerontion's knowledge becomes exclusively the forbidden knowledge of good and evil, tears "shaken from the wrath-bearing tree," in contrast to Christ, who belongs to "the juvescence of the year." Both poems move towards a self-recognition scene, a scene which is parody because it is the ego, the illusory self capable only of death, that is recognised.

Sweeney, as an *homme moyen sensuel*—or perhaps a trifle more than *moyen*—is more adapted to his world than Prufrock or Gerontion, which may be one reason why he is associated with animals. He is called "Apeneck Sweeney," is compared to a zebra, a giraffe and an orang-outang, and is clearly blood brother to "The Hippopotamus." We have noted his connexion with the Yahoo or pure natural man, and his role as the guardian of the "horned gate," of the true or high dream which

comes from Eden into experience, also associates him
with the original fall of man. But Sweeney has a more
likeable side, especially in *Sweeney Agonistes*. In this poem
the two extremes of existence, hell and heaven, are indicated by two epigraphs, one (repeated in *The Family
Reunion*) a speech of Orestes in Aeschylus and the other a
passage from St John of the Cross. Between these limits
Sweeney works out his own version of the two inner
worlds. Innocence is the "crocodile isle" that he proposes
taking Doris to, its embryonic withdrawal from life
symbolised by an egg. There follows a macabre story of a
man keeping a girl's corpse in a bathtub full of lysol, the
story being told not as a newspaper sensation but as a
parable of the kind of ordinary life that is indistinguish-
able from death. Sweeney is not haunted by furies like
Orestes or Harry Monchensey, and he is unlikely to get
far with St John of the Cross, but he is no fool, and his
troubled vision is something much more than a song for
simians.

The two Coriolan poems, "Triumpha! March" and
"Difficulties of a Statesman," are concerned with the
theme of heroism, in its traditional form—all Eliot's
other heroes are martyrs. Heroism, being a form of
energy in which no shadow falls between idea and
reality, belongs to innocence, but it can seek expression
only in experience, and its relation to experience is
normally tragic in consequence. Coriolanus, as the hero
of what Eliot calls Shakespeare's most successful play, is a
person of great integrity, but his inability to operate the
social machinery of tact and compromise keeps him imprisoned in that integrity. Thus he appears on two levels
of isolation, the isolation of the hero and the isolation of
the ego. We all know the latter kind, and occasionally it
catches an echo of the former, the "broken Coriolanus"
of *The Waste Land*. In "Triumphal March" Eliot's hero is
still genuinely detached, and a closer model for him than
Shakespeare's Coriolanus would be perhaps the Arjuna

of the *Bhagavadgita*, who is mentioned in "The Dry Salvages." In this work, an episode from the Indian epic *Mahabharata*, Arjuna finds himself on a battlefield fighting kinsmen, and has the kind of doubts about the value of what he is doing that Western heroes, including Coriolanus, are seldom afflicted with. His charioteer, the god Krishna in disguise, explains that as life is a battlefield, there is nowhere else to go, and eventually he reveals himself in a theophany, manifesting to Arjuna what Eliot calls in "Triumphal March" "the still point of the turning world," of which more later. But in "Difficulties of a Statesman," the inner paradise is breaking up and fading, the mother, so dominating and sinister a figure in Shakespeare, is beginning to replace it, the tone of parody deepens, and Coriolan is becoming less of a tragic hero and more of a victim.

There are several of these victim-figures in Eliot. The drowned Phoenician sailor Phlebas, who appears in "Dans le restaurant" and *The Waste Land*, has a strong feeling of Adonis about him, as his nationality suggests. In "Animula," which takes its name from the poem of Hadrian's already mentioned, the poet traces the life-cycle of unheroic man from birth to death, with echoes from Dante and Baudelaire, as a continuous distraction, no moment in it focussed in a state of real consciousness. This life is then contrasted with figures of energy, heroism or beauty cut down in fullness of life, who include another Adonis figure: "Floret, by the boarhound slain between the yew trees." With this line the mournful family of yews enters Eliot's poetry, to return in *Ash Wednesday* and *Four Quartets*. In "Burbank with a Baedeker" Eliot adopts the common Henry James situation of a fresh American innocence betrayed by a wily and venal Europe. Nothing very terrible happens to Burbank, but the overtones of Princess Volupine, besides her Jonsonian and Venetian name, are those of a macabre corpse-like Venus rising from the sea in the city of

Venus, of Cleopatra sitting on her barge, and perhaps of the blue-eyed hag Sycorax. Possibly even Sweeney, for all his broad bottom, may have enough exuberance and vitality to be a victim of the same type. At any rate some kind of sacrificial ritual seems to be building up around him in "Sweeney Among the Nightingales," although some readers feel that the atmosphere of this poem is that of a sexual dream, a sleeping contrast, or parallel, to "Sweeney Erect."

The only way to adjust perfectly to the dead-alive world is to be either a body without a mind, like the pneumatic Grishkin in "Whispers of Immortality," or a mind without a body, like the abstract entities that circumambulate her. In "Mr. Eliot's Sunday Morning Service" the opposition of Sweeney and the polymaths is less radical, but similar, and so is the opposition of the hippopotamus and the Laodicean church. Eliot's early imagery revolves around two figures: the youth or girl, killed or betrayed or deserted in fullness of life, and the weary old or middle-aged man who dreams of life in an after-dinner sleep—the phrase from *Measure for Measure* which forms the motto of "Gerontion." The latter group includes, besides Gerontion, Prufrock (not old, but, as Shaw says of one of his characters, one whom age cannot wither because he has never bloomed), Tiresias in *The Waste Land*, Simeon, glad to slip quietly out of the world before the sword of the Word enters it, and the bewildered Magi who would be "glad of another death." The speaker in "Lines for an old man," under whose sardonic and malevolent eye "The dullard knows that he is mad," is a considerably more vigorous type, said to have some connexion with Mallarmé. The former group (Phlebas, Burbank, Floret, La Figlia che Piange) belong to the world of innocence, and the image chiefly associated with them is that of water.

Experience is largely an accumulating of grime and corruption, and water is its cleansing agent. In "Dans le restaurant," as the waiter shuffles off to what the narrator hopes is a bath, we encounter Phlebas lying in the sea, and the effect is an appreciation of what Keats calls the sea's task of pure ablution. In *The Waste Land* the Thames carries the filth of London into the sea, where we meet Phlebas again, and the healing waters return as rain at the end, reminding us of the symbolism of baptism in Christianity. In "Mr. Eliot's Sunday Morning Service" the contrast of the "baptized God" and Sweeney shifting hams in his bath is parallel to the contrast in "Dans le restaurant" between the slobbering waiter and the rainy weather outside which is called "the beggars' washday." The theme of "death by water" contains by implication a theme of rebirth by water, hence the theme of parodied self-recognition in Prufrock and Gerontion may have its opposite too, and we should expect this opposite recognition also to be associated with water.

In Dante's encounter with Matilda it is the brilliance of Matilda's eyes (and later those of Beatrice) that particularly impresses Dante. By contrast, the hollow men feel the reproachful eyes of those who are in death's other kingdom, and dare not meet those eyes even in dreams, for they belong to a vision deeper than the "low dream" they have. Closely related to *The Hollow Men* are two poems which, with one of its sections, originally formed a group called "Doris's Dream Songs." One, "Eyes that last I saw in tears," speaks of a "division" from eyes that in this world are seen only without tears, and hence as mocking or derisive. In the other, "The wind sprang up at four o'clock," the dreamer seems to be entering death's other kingdom, seen as a river which takes on the form of "a face that sweats with tears." These are strange dreams for Sweeney's practical and not over-visionary paramour. The second one especially seems to suggest that death may be the point at which one enters a spiritual community, as birth is the point at which one enters the ordinary human one.

One of the places where the "shadow" of *The Hollow Men* is said to fall is between the essence and the descent, and perhaps in ascent the shadow of life in experience rejoins its substance. When Dante meets Matilda in Eden, he recovers his original state, as he would have been without the fall, hence the meeting with Matilda has in it the recognition of his original nature, as though he were ending his life where he began it, as though Matilda were a part of himself that he is rejoining. The rose-garden world is the world of the might-have-been, and our lives run in counterpoint to another life we might have lived if man had not fallen out of Eden. A passage from Shelley's *Prometheus Unbound* which suggests that man is simultaneously a substance and a shadow in different worlds, the two uniting at death, in language as well as imagery very close to Eliot, is quoted at a crucial point of *The Cocktail Party*.

The ironic parody of this theme has its literary ancestry too. In a ghost story of Henry James, *The Jolly Corner*, a man meets himself as he might have been, and this story is referred to in *The Family Reunion*. A rather similar ghost story by May Sinclair, *Where Their Fire is not Quenched*, is alluded to in *The Elder Statesman*. But the archetype of all such ironic recognition scenes is the encounter of Aeneas and Dido in Virgil's hell, where Aeneas receives what Eliot calls "the most telling snub in all poetry."[5] This scene in the *Aeneid* is a contrast to Aeneas's earlier meeting with his mother Venus, a line from which forms the epigraph to "La Figlia che Piange."

"La Figlia che Piange" represents the "beginning" of Eliot's symbolism; the "end," which is the same point, is represented by "Marina." Marina in Shakespeare was the daughter of a Phoenician sailor, whose reunion with her forms one of those long recognition scenes, usually involving a father, a daughter and a sea, that are characteristic of Shakespeare's late comedies.[6] In Eliot the narrator is "crossing the bar," setting out into the sea of death in a leaky boat which, like Gerontion's house, symbolises his own body. The evil creatures of the shadow-world he is leaving behind become "unsubstantial," the thrush, the bird of the "Burnt Norton" rose-garden, is calling him, and as the end of his life rejoins its beginning, "images return." He begins to remember his past life, as Phlebas "passed the stages of his age and youth" ("sa vie antérieure" in the French version, which establishes a more definite link with Baudelaire's "La vie antérieure," with its imagery of submarine reincarnation). Gradually, as the world "under sleep" begins to open up, with the whispering laughter of the children in the trees (for the sea is vanishing, as in the Biblical apocalypse, and the rose-garden is taking its place), a face takes shape, the bodily form of a new life.

The Waste Land is a vision of Europe, mainly of London, at the end of the First World War, and is the climax of Eliot's "infernal" vision. It appeared in 1922, just before the poet had reached thirty-five, the middle of life's journey, when Dante began the *Inferno*. The setting is civilisation in the winter of its discontent, and the images are those of the end of the natural cycle: winter, the "brown land," ruins (including the nursery-rhyme collapse of London Bridge and, in the notes, the proposed demolition of nineteen city churches), and the Thames flowing to the sea. This world is physically above ground but spiritually subterranean, a world of shadows, corpses and buried seeds. The inhabitants live the "buried life" (a phrase from "Portrait of a Lady") of seeds in winter: they await the spring rains resentfully, for real life would be their death. Human beings who live like seeds, ego-centrically, cannot form a community but only an aggregate, where "Each man fixed his eyes before his feet," imprisoned in a spiritual solitude that recalls the story of the death of Ugolino in Dante. Such lines as

"And if it rains, a closed car at four" associate human life with its vegetative metaphors.

Dante's journey through hell begins on Good Friday evening, and he emerges on the other side of the earth on Easter Sunday morning. Thus his journey fits inside the three-day rhythm of the redemption, where Christ is buried on Friday evening, descends to hell on Saturday, and rises on Sunday morning. Similarly in the first section of *The Waste Land*, "The Burial of the Dead," we sink into the lower world of the "unreal city," crowds streaming into it like the damned in Dante. Here Christ appears as Isaiah's "shadow of a rock in a weary land," before we descend to the shades below, or as the possible power of resurrection in Ezekiel's valley of dry bones. We remain in the underworld all through the next two sections, and then follows "Death by Water," evidently physical death, as burial in earth symbolises the physical life which is spiritual death. Physical death is the final judgment between the seeds who can understand the commands of the thunder and die to a new life, and those who merely die and are rejected, as the sterile seed is rejected by nature. The last section repeats the image of a streaming crowd, "hooded hordes swarming," an apocalypse in which the invisible presence of the risen Christ accompanies scenes of terror and chaos as the valley of dry bones becomes "an exceeding great army," as Ezekiel says.

Easter represents the end of a long period of religious symbolism in which a "dying god," a spirit representing the fertility of nature, was thought to die and rise again, usually in a three-day festival. The information about the cults of Adonis, Attis, Osiris, and others collected in Frazer's *Golden Bough* is referred to by Eliot in the notes. In these rites a red or purple flower was associated with the god's blood: this appears in the hyacinths of *The Waste Land* and perhaps the "belladonna" or deadly nightshade (as well as in the dogwood and judas of

"Gerontion," the lilacs of *Ash Wednesday*, and elsewhere). The death of Adonis was mourned by women representing the spirit of the earth, and the line "Murmur of maternal lamentation" associates this with the Biblical weeping of Rachel.

As later in *Four Quartets*, there is an elaborate imagery of the four elements. The cycle of water, from spring rains and the wet hair of the hyacinth girl to the Thames flowing out to sea, returning as the rains bringing new life to the parched land, is most prominent. According to Charles Lamb, Webster's "Call for the robin redbreast and the wren," and Shakespeare's "Full fathom five" are the great elegies of death by earth and water respectively in the language, and both are referred to in *The Waste Land*. In "The Fire Sermon" there is the implicit contrast between the St Augustine and Buddha who appear at the end, seeking "the fire that refines them" (the last line of Canto 26 of the *Purgatorio*), and those who are burning in their own lusts with heat but without light. The air is hidden in the "brown fog" of a London winter; it blows freshly towards home but leaves Tristan as far away as the Ancient Mariner or Ulysses; it stirs up and confuses the perfumes of the woman in "A Game of Chess"; it is the element of the fearful apparitions and mirages of the closing scenes. The Ovidian theme of metamorphosis, associated chiefly with Philomela's transformation to a bird, runs through the poem, and modulates into the swallow of the *Pervigilium Veneris*. The dissolving and reforming of physical elements suggest that the reality of which they are an appearance is a spiritual substance, the risen Christ.

Apart from Easter, the idea of a descent into hell came to Dante from the sixth book of the *Aeneid*, where Aeneas enters the lower world with the aid of a "golden bough" and the Cumaean Sibyl. Another story about the Cumaean Sibyl hanging in a jar between heaven and earth and wanting only to die, a most vivid image of the "nightmare life in death" which is Eliot's theme, is told by Petronius, and forms the motto of the poem. Another, or perhaps the same, Sibyl is said to have asked the gods for as many years to live as she held grains of sand in her hand, but forgot to ask for continuous youth, in other words real life. She may be behind the phrase "fear in a handful of dust." The Sibyl is parodied in *The Waste Land* by Madame Sosostris, with her fake Egyptian name and her "wicked pack of cards." Aeneas sees, besides Dido, the shades and a hell of torments, a further world of rebirth into new life.

Virgil in turn drew for his vision from the *Odyssey*, where Ulysses calls up the shades to consult Tiresias. *The Waste Land*, we are told in the notes, is a reverie of Tiresias, who has the same relation to it that Gerontion has to his poem, and whose hermaphroditic shadow-mind contains all the men and women who appear in it. Tiresias had been both a man and a woman, and was considered an authority on the pleasures of sexual intercourse from both points of view, but the production of children is beyond him, and all the sexual unions in the poem are as sterile as the waste land itself. Eliot leaves it to Pound, however, to elaborate the Odyssey scene in his first canto: *The Waste Land* is an intensely Latin poem, owing much more to Virgil and Ovid.

The contrasting figure to Tiresias is Phlebas, sailing (as we learn from "Dans le restaurant") to Britain in quest of tin, symbolising a commerce which continues in "Mr. Eugenides, the Smyrna merchant," whose "pocket full of currants" makes a startling pun on the "current" that picks the bones of Phlebas. Carthage was a Phoenician colony, the hereditary enemy of Rome (the naval battle of Mylae is referred to in passing), and from Carthage, a "cauldron of unholy loves," St Augustine, repeating the journey of Aeneas, went to Italy to become a Christian. He later returned to become bishop of nearby Hippo, and a note left by Joyce, "Eliot: Bishop of

Hippo," associates him neatly with the author of "The Hippopotamus."

In Virgil and Homer the motive for the underworld journey is to learn the future, the kind of knowledge ordinarily closed to mankind. Thus Ulysses in Homer wishes to know his personal fate, and is told that he will return home and eventually meet death from the sea, like Phlebas. A similar anxiety to know the future is gratified by Madame Sosostris, and "The Dry Salvages" later explains that a shoddy occultism pandering to man's desire to know his future is characteristic of sterile cultures. In *The Waste Land* the coming of Christianity represents the turning of Classical culture from its winter into a new spring, for the natural cycle is also associated with the cycles of civilisation. This may be one reason for the prominence of the poets, Virgil and Ovid, who were contemporary with Christ. Whatever future faces us today would, then, logically be connected with a second coming of Christ. The second coming, however, is not a future but a present event, a confronting of man with an immediate demand for self-surrender, sympathy and control, virtues which are primarily social and moral, and are preliminary to the Christian faith, hope and love. The London churches, St Magnus Martyr, St Mary Woolnoth, and others, stand like sentinels to testify to the presence of the risen Christ in the ruins of Europe.

Thus the underworld journey seems to be an initiation, a learning of mysteries. It is an old theory that the sixth book of the *Aeneid* is an allegory of initiation into Eleusinian mysteries, and a similar theory was applied to Shakespeare's *Tempest* by Colin Still in *Shakespeare's Mystery Play*, a book mentioned in Eliot's preface to Wilson Knight's *Wheel of Fire* and published the year before *The Waste Land*. The court party in *The Tempest* make, like Aeneas and Augustine, a journey to Italy from Tunis (identified with Carthage by Gonzalo); they are thrown on an island off the Italian coast and go through an experience there which brings them to self-knowledge and repentance. Ferdinand, the hero, mourns the drowning of his father, and finds him alive after all, while in wooing Miranda he has to appease and then be reconciled with Miranda's father. In Christianity, similarly, Christ as the second Adam succeeds but also redeems the first Adam, and appeases and is reconciled with his eternal Father. This similarity between the Christian myth and the structure of comedy will meet us in the plays. The recognition scene in *The Tempest* discovers Ferdinand playing chess with Miranda, a game which ends either in checkmate, the death of the king, or in stalemate, like the two unions in the second section of *The Waste Land* which is called "A Game of Chess." Here Miranda is replaced by two female wrecks, with bad nerves and bad teeth respectively, corresponding to the spiritual and physical narcoses symbolised by burial in earth and in water. The former is a "Lady of the Rocks" who has overtones of Dido, Cleopatra, Pope's Belinda, Keats's Lamia, the Great Whore of the Bible, and other stylish vixens; the latter has no literary splendours around her except a dim recall of the drowned Ophelia. Eliot's note on his title for this section refers to two plays of Middleton and does not mention *The Tempest*, but we cannot always trust Eliot's notes.

The Tempest uses the romance theme of the prince who comes to a strange land and marries its king's daughter. In stories of the St George and Perseus type the king is aged or suffering from a mysterious wound symbolising sexual impotence; the land he rules is therefore waste, on the principles of sympathetic magic, and it is ravaged by a sea-monster for the same reason. The hero kills the monster and succeeds to the kingdom. In the background is a nature myth of winter turning to spring, sea and snow turning to spring rain, age turning to youth, a sleeping beauty awakened by her prince charming. But if the monster *is* winter, the hero must enter and emerge from it, like Jonah in the Bible, must die himself and be reborn. There is no monster in Eliot, but there are vestiges of his open mouth in the references to "Dead mountain mouth of carious teeth" and "This decayed hole among the mountains." With the theme of death and revival the dragon-killer story merges with the dying-god story.

In some medieval versions of the same myth studied by Jessie Weston in *From Ritual to Romance*, cited by Eliot as a source for *The Waste Land*, the youthful knight comes to a waste land ruled by an aged and wounded "fisher king." Two mystical signs, a lance and a cup, are exhibited to him: had he asked their meaning the king would have been healed. Here the theme of descent and temporary death is represented by a "Chapel Perilous," an empty lighted chapel where the hero must pass a night while the lights are extinguished one by one. In the final section of *The Waste Land* the Chapel Perilous represents the underworld of death and burial, the tomb from which Christ rises. The lance and cup, originally fertility and sexual symbols, became associated with the lance of Longinus and the Holy Grail in the passion of Christ. They are to be connected also with the two red suits of the modern pack of cards, the diamond being a lance-head and the heart a chalice. Our cards are derived from a much more elaborate set, the Tarots, consulted by Madame Sosostris, which have twenty-two additional "trumps" with such names as the hanged man, the falling tower, death, the last judgment, and so on. Some of these, and others invented by Eliot, are mentioned in *The Waste Land*.

Another monster is slain by Jesus in his Easter victory over death and hell: the leviathan of the Old Testament, a sea-monster who *is* the sea, as he is death and hell, and also the devil, the serpent of Paradise, described in *The Rock* as "the great snake at the bottom of the pit of the world." In the Bible he or a similar monster is also identified with the kingdoms of tyranny, Egypt, Babylon, and the Phoenician city of Tyre. Thus the world that needs redemption is to be conceived as imprisoned in the monster's belly, whence the Messiah, following Jonah, descends to deliver it. In Christian iconography hell is often represented as an open-mouthed monster, from which Jesus emerges with the procession of the redeemed behind him, these forming a ghostly background to the final section of *The Waste Land*. The world to be redeemed is symbolically under water as well as under the earth, which gives point to the symbolism of fishing in the Gospels, and establishes a link with the "fisher king" of romance. Eliot's fisher king, sitting gloomily on the shore at the end of the poem with his "arid plain" behind him, thus corresponds to Adam, or human nature that cannot redeem itself. The progression of *bateaux ivres*, from Tristan's faraway ship to the "narrow canoe" of a girl's seduction, ending with the shipwrecked Phlebas, has the same relation to Adam that the responding boat, the symbol of the virtue of "control," has to the fisher of men who had the power to command the sea.

REFERENCES

1. "What is Minor Poetry?"
   O.P.P. p. 50.
2. "Ben Jonson," *S.E.* p. 158;
   "John Ford," *S.E.* p. 203.
3. "Matthew Arnold,"
   U.P.U.C. p. 106.
4. "Dante," *S.E.* p. 273.
5. "What is a Classic?" *O.P.P.*
   p. 62.
6. Cp. "John Ford," *S.E.* p. 194.

CHAPTER V

FROM FIRE BY FIRE

Eliot's later poems and the five plays, all of which are comedies or triumphant tragedies, belong to his "purgatorial" vision. *Ash Wednesday* (in six parts, numbered here for convenience) presents us with a desert, a garden, and a stairway between them. The stairway is the *escalina* or winding mountain of Dante's purgatory. In St John of the Cross the "dark night of the soul" is described as a spiritual dryness like that of a desert, and here again is a "ladder," equated with the "figure of the ten stairs" of St Benedict referred to in "Burnt Norton." St John also calls his purgation an "ascent of Mount Carmel," adding that it could also be called a descent, a remark bringing us toward Heraclitus' "the way up and the way down are the same." The stairway appears in the "infernal" vision in many ironic contexts, usually connected with failure in love. La Figlia che Piange stands "on the highest pavement of the stair"; the narrator in "Portrait of a Lady" nearly loses his precious "self-possession" at the top of his lady's stair; Prufrock wonders if there is time to turn back and descend the stair; the "young man carbuncular" climbs a staircase to the typist's flat; the narrators of "Rhapsody on a Windy Night" and "*The Boston Evening Transcript*" make their assignations with time and life at the top of steps: Princess Volupine climbs the water-stair to desert Burbank for Klein.

Desert and garden are central symbols in our literary and religious traditon, and a number of complexes of this symbolism have become so closely associated as to be readily identified. Seven of these, five from the Bible, one from Dante and one from the Church calendar, are identified in *Ash Wednesday*.

First, Adam, the "ruined millionaire," is condemned to earn his living in the wilderness, but is ultimately to be led back to Eden and have the tree and river of life restored to him. Second, Israel wanders in the desert forty years trying to enter its Promised Land, the Canaan they finally conquered being more of a desert than a garden, as is indicated by the desert setting of the line: "This is the land. We have our inheritance" (II). Third, there is Israel in its later exile, urged by the prophets to return and rebuild its temple. Jeremiah, finding no one to listen to him, was forced to cry: "O earth, earth, earth, hear the Word of the Lord." In *Ash Wednesday* "earth" is altered to "wind" (II), partly because the listening wind is associated with the Spirit inspiring the prophet. Isaiah speaks of the desert blossoming as the rose; Ezekiel in Babylon saw the valley of dry bones taking on the bodies of resurrection (II); Micah speaks the reproaches of the Word to a disobedient people (V). A later rebuilder of the temple, Nehemiah, figures in *The Rock*, but not here, where building imagery is not wanted. Fourth, there is the contrast, in two books ascribed to Solomon, between the world of vanity with "the burden of the grasshopper" in Ecclesiastes (II), and the garden of the Bride and her sister in the Song of Songs. St John of the Cross wrote his treatise on the dark night as a commentary on a poem based on the Song of Songs. In Eliot's garden there is a "Lady" (II), later a "veiled sister" (VI), who corresponds to Beatrice in Dante, besides the presence of the Virgin herself.

Fifth, the life of Christ is polarised between his temptation, where he wanders forty days in the desert, and his passion, which extends from the agony in the garden to his resurrection in another garden. In the Gospels, his ministry comes between these events, but in Biblical typology the temptation corresponds to the forty-year wandering of Israel in the desert under Moses, and the resurrection to the conquest of the Promised Land by Joshua, who has the same name as Jesus. Hence (sixth) the commemorating of the temptation by the Church in the forty days of Lent, which begins on Ash Wednesday, is immediately followed by the celebration of the resurrection in Easter. Finally, and seventh, Dante's *Purgatorio* takes us up a rocky mountain of penance into "our first world" of Eden.

The desert of *Ash Wednesday* is the "brown land" of the earlier poems, but, except for the references to "noise" in v, it is conceived not as a sterile society but as a shrivelled individual spiritual life, a chapel perilous or house of the dead. Its main features parallel and contrast with those of the garden world above it. It is "The place of solitude where three dreams cross" (VI), apparently the dreams of waking consciousness, memory, and dream proper, all of them animated by desire, all of them having no end but death. It is a place of thirst, in contrast to the fountains and springs of the garden, where water can only be miraculously provided, as it was to Moses and to Samson (the story of Samson's thirst may be glanced at in the line "The broken jaw of our lost kingdoms" in *The Hollow Men*).[1] Above the desert, the inhabitants of the garden have abandoned the "low dream" for the "higher dream," and memory for a life "In ignorance and in knowledge of eternal dolour" (IV). In Dante the river Lethe, which obliterates the memory of sin, and the river Eunoe, which restores unfallen knowledge, are in Eden. In Eliot's garden there can still be talk of "trivial" things (IV), the word being an erudite pun on the three-way crossing of ordinary life.

The three dreams appear in the second section as three leopards eating the body and leaving only the dry bones. We are reminded of the three beasts encountered by Dante at the beginning of the *Inferno* and of the world, flesh and devil, symbolised as three beasts, in St John of the Cross. The contrasting image is that of the unicorns, emblems of chastity and of Christ, drawing the "gilded hearse" of the body about to be glorified (IV). The limit of the desert is marked by two "blue rocks" (V), suggesting the clashing Symplegades of the Argonautic voyage, and that in turn suggesting the open-mouthed monster of hell, mentioned earlier. The limit of the garden is marked by two yew trees (IV, VI), apparently representing the spiritual death of the first two sections and the physical death which follows it. At the same time the scene of the poem is "The desert in the garden and the garden in the desert" (V); the two worlds occupy the same time and space.

The narrator is in middle life, beginning to realise that life is a parabola. He is not content however with the chagrin of ordinary experience: he wants to kill the ego, reduce it to scattered bones in a desert, pulverise it on Ash Wednesday into the dust from which it came. He descends from despair founded on disillusionment to despair founded on reality, the despair of finding anything in the past worth clinging to. The experiences worth clinging to are discontinuous, and pull one off the track of memory and desire. It is only when the narrator's very bones have stopped clinging together that he can become aware of any other reality, and his separating bones are in contrast to the prayer at the end: "Suffer me not to be separated" (VI). The leopards, however terrifying, are really agents of redemption, an ambiguity which meets us often in the plays.

The poet, in climbing his stairway, looks down to see that he has been detached from his temporal self. The Jacob who dreamed of the ladder to heaven also wrestled with the angel, and the poet sees himself, "the same shape" (III), in a lower world fighting the demon of hope and despair. He then sees more clearly that he is escaping from "the toothed gullet of an aged shark" (III), like

Jonah, or Dante from hell. The glances below are followed by a vision on his own level, where the world of memory and desire suddenly reappears in the form of a dancing Pan figure, and where the memories of "Lilac and brown hair" (III) suggest that we are in the world of the hyacinth girl and La Figlia che Piange. Finally we reach the garden, where Pan is reduced to a statue with a "breathless" flute (IV), and where we meet the greater recognition scene hinted at in "Marina":

> One who moves in the time between sleep and
> waking, wearing
> White light folded, sheathed about her, folded.

Ordinary consciousness reasserts itself, and we are back (V) in the desert, like Elijah, who sat down under a "juniper tree" (II) and prayed to die. The juniper tree is also associated with a resurrection from bones in a fairy tale of Grimm.[2] Elijah, after earthquakes and thunder, heard the still small voice of the Word, but the poet is in a world of constant noise and distraction which is determined not to listen. So although the poem begins with renunciation, "Because I do not hope to turn again" (I), it ends with the world of memory and desire stronger than ever: "Although I do not hope to turn again" (VI). The "unbroken wings" (VI) of sailing ships mock the "aged eagle" (I) who cannot renew his youth, and "the empty forms between the ivory gates" (VI) of illusory dreams come to him with the unbearable beauty of a lost paradise.

The experiences in *Ash Wednesday* take place on four levels: the level of spiritual vision or high dream in III and IV; the level of nostalgic vision in VI; the level of ordinary experience, of disillusionment and distraction, in I and V, and the level of ascesis or self-denial in II. The first level is a world of identity, where the individual is identified with his community, a member of one body, without losing his individuality:

The single Rose
Is now the Garden
Where all loves end (ii).

The second level is a world where experiences of peculiar
intensity are linked by memory and impose a pattern of
greater significance and sadness on ordinary life—very
like the *temps retrouvé* of Proust. The third level is ordinary
experience, where the ego tries to achieve identity through
"memory and desire" and the fourth level is the concen-
trating of consciousness designed to break up the illusions
of the ego. These four levels recur in the Quartets.

A book this size has no space for full commentary on
Four Quartets, and some "audio-visual aids" will have to
do instead. Draw a horizontal line on a page, then a
vertical line of the same length cutting it in two and
forming a cross, then a circle of which these lines are
diameters, then a smaller circle inside with the same centre.
The horizontal line is clock time, the Heraclitean flux,
the river into which no one steps twice. The vertical line
is the presence of God descending into time, and crossing
it at the Incarnation, forming the "still point of the
turning world." The top and bottom of the vertical line
represent the goals of the way up and the way down,
though we cannot show that they are the same point in
two dimensions. The top and bottom halves of the larger
circle are the visions of plenitude and of vacancy respectively; the top and bottom halves of the smaller circle
are the world of the rose-garden and (not unnaturally for
an inner circle) of the subway, innocence and experience.
(Subway is, to me at any rate, "The familiar word exact
without vulgarity," though if one had the freedom of
Finnegans Wake one could describe Eliot's inner circle as
a "tuberose.") What lies below experience is ascesis or
dark night. There is thus no hell in *Four Quartets*, which
belong entirely to the purgatorial vision.

In each Quartet there are five sections, all except the

fourth divided into two parts by theme, and usually by metre as well, making nine parts in all. Two parts, iv and iia, are lyrical; the rest is in a meditative style, which sometimes, especially in iii, becomes deliberately prosaic. Subject to a principle of context to be explained in a moment, all four poems have much the same structure and narrative movement. We begin (ia) on the horizontal line of time, in a mood and with imagery that set the tonality for that poem. Then we go on to a vision of plenitude (ib) which in three of the Quartets is reached through a "loop in time" (a phrase from *The Family Reunion*), and is associated with the past. There follows (iia) a lyric which brings the emotional impact of this vision into focus. Then we come to the awareness of the present moment (iib), the centre of our diagram, thence to ordinary experience (iiia), thence to a withdrawal from ordinary experience (iiib), which takes us into a lyrical "dark night" vision (iv). Then comes a passage dealing with or alluding to the relation of art to human experience (va), and a final resolution in the tonality with which we began (vb).

"Burnt Norton," the first Quartet, is an apocalyptic poem, and gives us a bird's-eye view of the whole range of experience covered in its successors. In *The Waste Land* there were two descents, one into earth, symbolising ordinary experience, and one into water, then an upward turn anticipated by a "fire sermon." Similarly, after "Burnt Norton," we descend into the muddy and practical world of "East Coker," then into the water of "The Dry Salvages." There we realise that, like Dante after he passed the centre of the world at the end of the *Inferno*, we are travelling, emotionally speaking, in the opposite direction. In the last two Quartets what corresponds to the earlier visions of the "way up" (ib and iia) are vision of loss and despair: it is the "dark night" lyric (iv) that is the focus of hope. "Burnt Norton" trails off rather plaintively at the end, but "Little Gidding" begins in a mood of penance and takes us back to the rose-garden with which "Burnt Norton" began. Thus the four Quartets form a single cycle that begins and ends at the same point.

The archetype of this cycle is the Bible, which begins with the story of man in a garden. Man then falls into a wilderness or waste land, and into a still deeper chaos symbolised by a flood. At the end of time he is restored to his garden, and to the tree and water of life that he lost with it. But by that time the garden has become a city as well, a fiery city glowing with gold and precious stones, so that the tree of life (symbolised in Dante by a rose) is a tree in which "the fire and the rose are one."

On the horizontal line of time, where we are dragged backwards into an unknown future facing the past, the primary emotion is anxiety. Efforts to find clues in the past that will make the future more predictable range from a "popular" (i.e. progressive) belief in evolution to tea-cup reading, but in any case:

> Men's curiosity searches past and future
> And clings to that dimension.

The past is no more reassuring than the future: the mouth of hell, we could almost say, is the previous moment, when what was up to then possible passes forever into an unchangeable past. Or, if not the mouth of hell, it is certainly the mouth of death, nibbling off our lives like the leopards in *Ash Wednesday*, and we feel (though in the opposite sense from the one intended in the context) that "the time of death is every moment." The egocentric life breeds panic, and panic breeds attachment, the clutch of the drowning man. In thought, attachment eventually leads to superstition, and every man becomes superstitious when he is sufficiently frightened.

Most of us take a less conscious view of time, because we are impelled by a natural force which Eliot calls desire, and which keeps us going like a train moving

"In appetency, on its metalled ways." We get used to riding backwards; there is a constant change of scene, and consequently a possibility of unbroken distraction. As we get older and our powers fail, we enter the world of boredom, and move from the anxieties of Prufrock to the indifference of Gerontion. Here we lose our sense of attachment, but not the egocentric core of it, and gain nothing except perhaps a "deliberate hebetude." One has to be sure of being kept firmly under sedation at all times if such a life is to be tolerable.

The fact which presses in on consciousness is the necessity for a detachment that is not merely indifference. There seems to be a constant cycle turning in time and nature, but nothing exactly repeats itself. We learn little if anything from past experience, because every situation is a new one. We get hurt in experience, and change so rapidly that we have the illusion of being healed by time, but the hurt remains if we do not. Our dreams and ambitions are continually being wrecked on some sunken rocks hidden in our past lives. It is easier to see this with others than with ourselves, and diagnosing the limitations of others is one of our favorite amusements.

A curious paradox is involved here. In the first place, it is true that "time is no healer: the patient is no longer here." But at the same time there is a healing factor in the very change of patient. We find a continuous vitality in ourselves which "Sings below inveterate scars," and prevents those of us who are not hopeless neurotics from revolving around the same point. The same paradox applies to the future. It is not hard to see why we are told in the Gospels not to take thought for the morrow. It is obvious that nothing we do will have the results we intend it to have. Our intentions drift off into the land of the might have been, and posterity sees them as nostalgic memories, vicarious rose-gardens. Yet without some commitment, some feeling that something will be here when we are not, it would be hard to find a standard that would make one line of conduct better than another.

The resolution of the paradox begins in a detachment which rejects the continuity of time. The moments of our life are discontinuous, and relate to another dimension of life altogether. Nothing remains of our past lives, yet we are convinced that we are the same person we were earlier, and this continuum of identity is the solid bottom of experience, the foundation we can build on. Our building materials are the continuous institutions, more particularly the Church, which make up our human home. The structure we find ourselves inhabiting is an identity that is in time but somehow not of it, a present moment which, unlike most present moments, is not chained by desire and anxiety to past and future:

> This is the use of memory:
> For liberation—not less of love but expanding
> Of love beyond desire, and so liberation
> From the future as well as the past.

It is easy to imagine a God above time who can see the whole continuum at once, as a man in an aeroplane can see a bend in the road concealed to the pedestrian. But a timeless God is of no use to us, and a temporal God would be as much in the flux as we are. Christianity presents us with the conception of a timeless God substantially entering time, a paradoxical and "impossible union" which was achieved once for all by the Incarnation, and is repeated every day in the Church's sacrament. But the entry into time was also an entry into each one of us, making it possible for us to live in this impossible union of two existences, if only for brief instants. This is a conception which gives a different meaning, not simply to life, but to every moment in the experience of life. Every moment is potentially the "still point of the turning world," the apprehension of a real present and a real presence in time and space, which is ourselves and yet annihilates everything that we habitually call our-selves.

Nobody but a saint could make such moments of apprehension continuous, or even frequent. Most of us have moments of a greater than ordinary awareness, but do not know what to do with them, or what their real significance is. In a world where the "shadow" of *The Hollow Men* falls "between the emotion and the response," we usually have the awareness first and the consciousness of having had it follows later. But whether an instant later or many years later, the consciousness comes to a different person. The reality of all such moments, "The hint half guessed, the gift half understood, is Incarnation." In an early "Prelude," the poet, surveying a "blackened street," is "moved by fancies" which take the form of

> The notion of some infinitely gentle
> Infinitely suffering thing.

In that context, of course, this could be nothing more than a "notion," but even so it is described in terms which make it clear what its reality would be if that reality were grasped. The recognition of the presence of God in the world is the central spiritual act: the self-recognition glanced at in the previous chapter depends on it. Its product is sanctity, or life with a sacramental shape, con-formed to the pattern of what is above human life. Such sanctity is the only form of wisdom that is not based ultimately on illusion.

In "Burnt Norton" we begin (1a) with the horizontal line of time. The most natural intellectual way of unify-ing time is through complete fatalism. A foreordained future has in a sense already happened, so the present moment is real in the sense that it is the same as every other moment. The opening of "Burnt Norton," in a heavy rhythm like soldiers marching through mud, tells us that "perhaps" all time is *chronos* or clock-tick, in which everything will disappear and be "unredeem-able." In this grim philosophy there is no place for a "might have been," for nothing could have happened except what did happen. But nobody's life is like this: we all have doors to little secret gardens in which, as Harry says in *The Family Reunion*, "what did not happen is as true as what did happen." After the transient rose-garden vision (1*b*), there follows (11*a*) a lyric which brings its vision into focus as a larger vision of plenitude in the form of correspondence, all the levels of the chain of being from stars to mud revolving around a "bedded axle-tree," the last word being a common Elizabethan term for the mechanism on which the universe turns. The stars, the seasons, the organic rhythms of the body, form interlocking patterns in a cosmic dance like that of the *Paradiso* or Davies' *Orchestra*. The image of hunter and hunted on earth being "reconciled" among the stars, as so frequently at the end of Ovid's tales of meta-morphosis, is met earlier in an ironic form in "Sweeney Among the Nightingales," where the hunting of Sweeney is preceded by the veiling of "Gloomy Orion and the Dog."

We now start on our way down, first to the crossing point or the present moment (11*b*). This, in "Burnt Norton," is time in the sense of the Biblical *kairos*, as distinct from *chronos*; the present and presence of a Logos neither timeless nor temporal, but now and for-ever. One is aware of assuming a double part here, of being neither in nor out of time, but in a state of *Erhebung*, an exaltation which is not clear of its origin but is rather a hovering or brooding state like that of the Spirit on chaos, or the poet "seeking the beginning and the end" of his poem.

The awareness of the present moment carries us through ordinary experience (111*a*), symbolised by the London tube, in detachment. But for the "way down" we must go deeper (111*b*), into the dark night of the chapel perilous, the state of ascesis symbolised by death in the grave (IV) with the yew tree bending over us, too far away from the sun or the sunflower to turn to us. Here we realise, not simply that the Logos is in death as well as life, but that "the moment of the rose and the moment of the yew-tree Are of equal duration," that the top of the way up, the bottom of the way down, and the still point in the middle, are all in the same place.

In the final section (Va) art takes its place, in the way explained earlier, as a technique of meditation, showing by its form how the beginning and the end can be in the same time. "Burnt Norton" puts a considerable stress on the "formal pattern," the dance of life which is both movement and form, a state of becoming which is not merely liquid and a state of being which is not merely solid. This combination of movement and form is equally present in all the arts, whether they present themselves in time like music or in space like pottery. But the conception of life as a dance or formal pattern manifested by art can easily become glib and facile unless we realise that the foundations of the palace of art are built on the shifting sands of the waste land. The conception itself, though easy to formulate, cannot be realised except at rare moments. For practically the whole of life we are standing in a "Ridiculous" waste desert (Vb) when the voices of the children in the rose-garden are as mocking and more elusive than the "shrieking voices" of the desert itself.

In "Burnt Norton" we are not confused by the incongruity of "Garlic and sapphires in the mud" because we are watching the cosmic patterns that form on the turning wheel. In "East Coker" we get into the mud, the ordinary world of confusion, and the tone is more sombre and realistic. The discussion of the arts (Va) is concerned not with their formal perfection but with the poet's struggles with words. The present moment (IIb) is here only a moment at which one realises that nothing can be expected from past or future. The sense of ordinary experience (IIIa) is correspondingly more gloomy: here the recall of the underground train is in the middle of an *ubi sunt* elegy on the disappearance of all things in time. The close of this part of the poem (IIIb) is a passage based on St John of the Cross, but recalling some of the contradictions associated with the world of appearance by Bradley.

What corresponds in "East Coker" to the rose-garden and yew tree of "Burnt Norton" (Ib and IV) are two visions of marking time by the repetition of ritual. In the former we have a midsummer night dance of country peasants, which the poet again stumbles on through a loop in time, an instinctive response to the cycles of the seasons and human life, with the innocence of a community unawakened to self-consciousness. The dark night vision is that of the sacraments of the Church, where the bleak hospital imagery, the pedantic allegory, the concentration on Good Friday, and the harsh whether-you-like-it-or-not dogmatism are in sharp and consistent contrast. The "East Coker" counterpart to the vision of correspondence (IIa) is a natural apocalypse, the sense of time stretching out from winter to the returning ice-age. In the "East Coker" context of humility and concern with the present moment this kind of vision is out of key: there is a pretentious "I accept the universe" feeling about it that the poet turns his back on (IIb).

"East Coker" is, by virtue of its theme and context, a more personal poem than "Burnt Norton." Burnt Norton is, we are told, the name of a country house in Gloucester which was burned in the eighteenth century. Its connexion with the poem does not, to put it mildly, leap to the eye, beyond a very vague suggestion of the home of a "ruined millionaire." But East Coker was the place from which the Eliots left for Massachusetts in the seventeenth century, and the return of the poet, as an Anglo-Catholic and naturalised British subject, to his own historical embryo, so to speak, provides the reversible motto, said to have been that of Mary Queen of Scots, "In my end is my beginning," for the poem. An earlier Thomas Elyot, author of the sixteenth-century treatise *The Gouvernour*, is quoted in the country dance section. Thus the poem moves toward the kind of self-recognition that we have met already in other contexts in Eliot. The poet's natural life follows the cycle of nature around to its end in the sea in the final lines of the poem, and its focussing points are the moments of frustration and impotence behind which is:

> . . . echoed ecstasy
> Not lost, but requiring, pointing to the agony
> Of death and birth.

"The Dry Salvages" is the most explicit of the Quartets, and its surface meaning should cause little difficulty if the main ideas of the four poems have been grasped. Although the railway train, above ground this time, reappears (III*b*), horizontal time is conceived rather as a driving power that shakes and pounds us with its rhythm, filling our lives with desire and our minds with distraction. This power is symbolised by the cycle of water, which begins with old man river, the flooding Mississippi that flows past Eliot's birthplace, of which the plenitude or fulfilment is the ocean. The beauty of the great reverie on the sea (I*b*) does not conceal the sense of terror and waste, manifest in the grotesque junkpile of "dry salvage" (the pun is implicit in the title) it spews up on shore. We are back to the fisher king of *The Waste Land*. In the following lyric (II*a*), an adapted sestina, the sense of *de profundis*, of human life crying like Jonah from the belly of hell, deepens and intensifies. The dialectical symbols for the poem suggest Henry Adams. At one extreme we have the "worshippers of the machine," building bridges across the Mississippi and forgetting its potential dangers until it floods. The sinister warning sounds that keep the time of the ocean, the clang of the foghorn and the "groaner" that echo the terrors of fishermen's wives, modulate into the "angelus" in a prayer to the Virgin. This leads the theme of sinking into the sea into images of absorption, and those in turn lead to the apprehension of a real presence (the Incarnation is explicitly named in this poem). The arts appear (va) only in a reference to hearing music so deeply that absorption becomes identification.

Little Gidding was a seventeenth-century community of Anglican contemplatives, and symbolises, like East Coker in a different way, the poet's return to the point in history at which, for him, the modern world began. In "East Coker" an Eliot who is now an Anglo-Catholic and British subject returns to the point of his beginning and end; in "Little Gidding" he visits the place that Charles I, the "broken king," also visited during his defeat by Parliament. The Nazi air-raids have begun, and it is clearly time to end the Civil War; hence allusions to the seventeenth century form part of a general amnesty in which Cavalier and Roundhead are "folded in a single party." The water imagery of "The Dry Salvages" is horizontal; in "Little Gidding" the dominant image is fire, which moves vertically. The presence of the Logos is symbolised by a fire descending from heaven, the fire of divine love which kindles a human love springing up in response. The divine fire is the "pentecostal fire" (1a), the tongues of flame which were the Holy Spirit, the "Dove descending" (iv) on the apostles. The human fire is represented by Hercules (iv), who in the agony of his poisoned shirt kindled a funeral pyre and ascended to heaven on it, one of the few human beings accepted by the Classical gods. Here the dialectic of communion and moments of agony, emergent in "The Dry Salvages," is completed. The imagery is parodied by the Nazi bombing plane (called, in a figure more symmetrical than fortunate, the "dark dove"), and the answering fires breaking out of the "disfigured street" in London.

Many seventeenth-century writers were fascinated by a curious experiment of burning a flower, usually a rose, to ashes and seeing the ghost of the flower hovering over the ashes, which apparently afforded a dubious argument for immortality, or, at least, the permanence of things in time. Yeats says he tried this experiment without results. In "Little Gidding" the "spectre of the Rose" cannot be summoned by any return to the past, and the "burnt roses" leave nothing but "Ash on an old man's sleeve." Yet at the end the rose-garden of "Burnt Norton" (the title of this poem is becoming more significant) reappears, not only unharmed by the fire like the three men in Daniel, but itself on fire, a burning bush never consumed. We move from the endless destruction of physical substance (IIa)—Heraclitus speaks of the elements dying each other's lives, living each other's deaths—to the eternity of spiritual substance, "A condition of complete simplicity," attained only by the holocaust of everything in time, the reborn phoenix.

The "loop in time" here (Ib) is the poet's visit to Little Gidding and his feeling of communication with the dead, a communication "tongued with fire," a tradition recreated in individual experience. This communication materialises in the present moment (IIb) of a London air-raid, where the poet meets "a familiar compound ghost," the body of his poetic teachers in one form, from Dante to Ezra Pound, like Dante himself meeting his master Brunetto Latini in hell, which the burning London street resembles. The poet "assumed a double part" so that he was both talking to the master and watching himself being talked to. The talker, who is wholly involved in the state of experience, gets little encouragement beyond a prophecy of failing powers and growing disillusionment. There is a suggestion of Palinurus about the ghost, and we recall Eliot's remark about Aeneas: "*His*

reward was hardly more than a narrow beachhead and
a political marriage in a weary middle age."³ But the
watcher has achieved the detachment in ordinary
experience (IIIa) that is not to be compared with mere
disillusionment. We are travelling in the opposite direction from "Burnt Norton," and the poet's self-detach-
ment leads (IIIb), not to the "world of perpetual solitude,"
but to acceptance and reconciliation, a "lifetime burning
in every moment." Sin itself is "Behovely"—meaning,
roughly, that it is a kind of negative tribute to human
dignity—and sooner or later the human tragedy is consumed in the divine comedy. History, like the lives that
make it up, becomes "a pattern of timeless moments,"
and the significant acts of history, such as martyrdoms,
merge into the significant words of poetry (Va), both of
which are, as Dante says, "Legato con amor in un
volume,"⁴ bound up by Love into the Book of the Word.

The word "comedy" applies to stories with a happy
ending. A young man and woman are in love, their
love is thwarted, and some twist in the plot brings them
together, reconciles parents or exposes villains, and creates
a happier society assumed to begin as soon as the play
ends. In a comedy's end is its beginning. The end restores what the audience has seen all along to be the
desirable state of affairs, hence in a comedy's beginning
is its end.

This kind of comedy is cyclical, confined to Eliot's two
inner worlds. A younger generation normally outwits
an older one, and we feel a sense of rebirth and a new
state of innocence growing out of the play's experience.
There is another kind of comedy where the complica-
tions in front of the happy ending become tragic, so that
the comedy contains a tragedy instead of avoiding one.
The Christian myth, where Christ appeases the wrath
of his Father and becomes the Bridegroom of his redeemed
Church, who is both a Bride and a new society, is a

"divine comedy" in which the two greatest tragedies, the fall of man and the Crucifixion, are episodes. Some profound comedies, such as the late plays of Shakespeare, also contain tragic actions instead of avoiding them, and throw the emphasis on reconciliation and forgiveness rather than on a happy ending. Some Greek tragedies put the tragic action within a larger action that concludes in a tone of serenity or even happiness. There are four such tragedies in Greek drama, Aeschylus' *Eumenides*, Sophocles' *Oedipus at Colonus*, Euripides' *Alcestis* and Euripides' *Ion*, and each has been an important influence on one of Eliot's plays.

In *Murder in the Cathedral* the dialectical and purgatorial aspect of the Christian "comic" action is at its clearest. The foreground action is a tragedy in which the hero knows that

> . . . all things
> Proceed to a joyful consummation.

Of the four worlds, there is no place for the rose-garden: we begin in experience, represented by the chorus. The chorus becomes increasingly aware that experience is the doorway of hell, and as the murderers move closer the women of Canterbury are haunted by images of beasts of prey, filth and corruption, ending in the cry: "The Lords of Hell are here." Meanwhile Becket is immediately involved in a sequence of temptations. The chorus describes him as "unaffrayed among the shades," and he says himself, in language recalling the *Purgatorio* line "Treating shadows as a solid thing":

> . . . the substance of our first act
> Will be shadows, and the strife with shadows.

The first tempter, "Leave-well-alone," presents a temptation that Becket has gone too far to yield to even if he were capable of it. Its object however is not to persuade him to desert, but merely to remain in his mind as a source of distraction, confusing him in crucial moments:

> Voices under sleep, waking a dead world,
> So that the mind may not be whole in the present.

Temptations of compromise and of intrigue follow, but the dangerous temptation is an unexpected fourth one to "do the right deed for the wrong reason": to persevere in integrity and die a glorious martyr's death. This temptation is really an act of grace, something that Becket would never even have encountered by himself, much less overcome. The fact that the fourth tempter, as he leaves, repeats, word for word, Becket's opening speech in the play, indicates that Becket at this point has "assumed a double part," separating his real immortal self from the unpurified part of himself. Both this theme and the theme of something apparently demonic turning out to be an agent of grace are frequent in the other plays.

Murder in the Cathedral falls into two parts, each leading up to a prose speech addressed to the audience, a little like the parabasis in Aristophanes. The first speech is Becket's sermon after he has overcome the conflict in his mind and is awaiting martyrdom; the second is an apology for his murder made by the murderers. One is the voice of reason accommodating revelation to human ears; the other is the voice of rationalisation accommodating a criminal act to public opinion. The first part, the conflict of Becket with temptation, is the dramatic action properly speaking, and the action of the second part, the external conflict between Becket and his murderers, is the completing of it.

In *The Family Reunion*, Harry, Lord Monchensey, returns to his mother's house, significantly named Wishwood, to meet her and an assemblage of relatives on her birthday. Harry is, like the women of Canterbury, haunted by a sense of latent evil hiding behind his life. His wife was drowned at sea, and he says he pushed her overboard, but nobody believes him. He says that for the feeling he has "the particular has no language": he can express it only in symbols of guilt, but in itself it is closer to the "origin of wretchedness," or original sin. If nothing changed in time, one might repeat an earlier experience, and Harry might find his other self in boyhood at home, his counterpart in the rose-garden. But, as his aunt Agatha foresees, his self-recognition is of the ironic kind, as in Henry James' story *The Jolly Corner*, to which she refers. What happens is the opposite: Harry's haunting sense of evil is objectified at Wishwood in the form of the Furies. These are the beings he has fled from as he comes back to his rose-garden world, only to find that they are directly in front of him there, threatening cherubim over his Eden. He now sees that he must pursue them, that he cannot escape the guilt they symbolise but must accept it as the basis of a wider understanding. He must think, not "there they are," but "here they are." Thus the Furies, like Becket's last temptation, are really a gift of grace: they are hounds of heaven or agents of the dark night. They turn into "bright angels," and he goes off to an unknown destiny.

Harry is not an attractive character, and he may be, as Eliot says later, something of a prig.[5] He goes from absorption in one kind of self to absorption in another kind, and from the outside it is hard to know whether he is saintly or selfish. In particular, it is not clear why his enlightenment should force him to leave Wishwood: the word "missionary" is dropped, anticipating a theme of *The Cocktail Party*, but not developed. Then again, in any play which recalls the *Oresteia*, the dramatist is in duty bound to introduce the theme of a family "curse": the theme is introduced, but does not give the concluding action much sharpness of outline. Still, Harry's action makes his Wishwood another Chapel Perilous in which one must die to be reborn. In the original Chapel Perilous the lights of the chapel are gradually extinguished during the knight's vigil: this rite is performed on the candles of his mother Amy's birthday cake, while Amy, all her hopes for Wishwood annihilated by Harry's refusal to stay there, is dying offstage.

The main themes of all Eliot's plays are present in this one. There is a central figure who goes through a spiritual purgation and attains a vision of the four worlds, being isolated from the other characters and most of the audience in the process. There is something of this theme even in *Sweeney Agonistes*, and Eliot elsewhere speaks of it as a central interest of his in drama. In three of the five plays this enlightenment cuts the central figure off from marriage, and in the other two there is no question of marriage. There is also a subordinate group of those who, without full enlightenment, manage to achieve enough detachment to live a real life, and this is the level for which marriage, or a renewed understanding in an old marriage, seems to be appropriate. It is represented by the Chamberlaynes in *The Cocktail Party*, by the Mulhammers and their progeny in *The Confidential Clerk*, by Monica and Charles Hemington in *The Elder Statesman*. In *The Family Reunion* we have only Mary on this level, and Mary, left without matrimonial prospects when Harry fixes his eyes on the horizon, is forced to be content (though she seems so) with a fellowship in a women's college. The theme of a son imitating his father's career point for point is in three of the plays, and the somewhat oracular role of Agatha as a spiritual guardian recurs in the blessing ritual in *The Cocktail Party* and, more farcically, in the Mrs Guzzard of *The Confidential Clerk*. The Chapel Perilous is represented by a "sanatorium" in *The Cocktail Party* and *The Elder Statesman*.

In *The Cocktail Party* there are some references to Euripides' *Alcestis*, which explain both the allegorical meaning of the "sanatorium" as a house of death and the fact that Harcourt-Reilly, the psychiatrist whose role corresponds to Euripides' Heracles, sings like a drunk in the first act and talks like a priest with the keys of death and hell in the second one. At the beginning, Edward Chamberlayne, deserted by his wife Lavinia, is giving a cocktail party unwillingly, to the guests he could not put off. He has the selfishness of Euripides' Admetus, but Lavinia is no Alcestis. Reilly, who has crashed the party, convinces Edward that he must have Lavinia back by the simple manoeuvre of telling him how lucky he is without her. Some fairly ruthless play therapy completes the cure, and in the final scene they are giving another cocktail party together, as an act of free choice. Thus the cocktail party symbolises Eliot's lesser initiation, the emergence from the world of Dante's Canto 3 into ordinary daylight.

Celia, the heroine, gets a profounder sense of original sin, and of the spiritual isolation that accompanies it. Looked at from this point of view, there is no human community at all: each individual is alone by himself, and alienated from God. The sense of sin, which is equally personal and impersonal, is too oppressive for Celia to reconcile herself to the human condition like the Chamberlaynes, and she starts on a spiritual journey which takes her into an austere nursing order, thence to martyrdom by crucifixion in Africa. The journey is described in terms recalling the Lady in *Comus*: Celia's humility and innocence makes her spiritually invulnerable, for all the physical horror of her death. Harcourt-Reilly tells us that he realised, in a premonition, that Celia would die a violent death, and the important question was which self she would be committed to at the moment of her death. Martyrdom, especially a hideous one, carries with it an unanswerable (and perhaps unfair) authority, and when the news of Celia's crucifixion is communicated to the others Edward says:

—If this was right for Celia—
There must be something else that is terribly
   wrong,
And the rest of us are somehow involved in the
   wrong.

The answer, that "every moment is a fresh beginning," echoes the Quartets.

The Confidential Clerk turns on the ancient device of the recognition scene, where hero or heroine discover their long-lost parents. There are seven characters, four in an older generation, Sir Claude Mulhammer, his wife Lady Elizabeth, his "confidential clerk" Eggerson, the pivot of the dramatic action, and Mrs Guzzard, who has a role like that of Buttercup in *Pinafore*. These four sit around a table and identify their offspring among the other three: Colby Simpkins, the hero and Eggerson's successor as confidential clerk, Lucasta Angel, the heroine, and B. Kaghan, who marries her. Mrs Guzzard, the dealer in this curious poker game, assigns Simpkins to herself, though both Sir Claude and Lady Elizabeth are convinced that he is a son of theirs by a previous liaison, and he finally goes off in a foster-son relationship to Eggerson. Thus everybody of the older generation in the play claims him as a son, though his real father, the late Mr Guzzard, does not appear. Lady Elizabeth's son is Kaghan and Lucasta is Sir Claude's daughter.

The atmosphere of demure farce is sustained throughout, and, as the hero remarks rather dazedly, everybody seems to have a heart of gold. The plot-complications are closer to Menandrine New Comedy than to *Ion* (to which however New Comedy owed a good deal), and still closer to Wilde's *Importance of Being Ernest*, though it lacks the exuberance of Wilde ("marry into a waiting-room, and contract an alliance with a parcel?"). The word "farce" reminds us of the high respect for farce that Eliot shows in his dramatic essays, where he speaks of it as the crea-

tion of a distorted but self-consistent world, found in
Rabelais, Dickens, and even Marlowe.[6] *Sweeney Agonistes*,
with its pounding jazz rhythms and its weird expres-
sionistic staging, is farce in this sense. *The Confidential
Clerk* is a different kind of farce, a comedy in which the
structure has been deliberately over-complicated, and so
turned up one notch from the conventional well-made
play into a parody of such a play.

The imagery of this comedy is confined to the inner
worlds, here symbolised by the suburban garden and the
"City," and the upper world is entered by marriage. Sir
Claude has for his "secret garden" a frustrated desire to
be a potter. Simpkins falls into the same pattern as long
as he believes himself to be Sir Claude's son, though his
ambition is to be an organist. Unlike Marvell, Simpkins
is not satisfied to be in his garden alone:

> If I were religious, God would walk in my garden
> And that would make the world outside it real
> And acceptable, I think.

This remark indicates a possibility of further growth in
him. He resents the fact that he will never be a first-rate
organist, but when he learns that his real father was a
frustrated organist too, humility comes to his aid and he
becomes an organist on his own level. Like Harry, he
transfers allegiance from one self to another, hence
Lucasta can say:

> ... You're either an egotist
> Or something so different from the rest of us
> That we can't judge you.

The Elder Statesman, which could be performed by the
same seven actors needed for its predecessor, returns us,
in a domestic and familiar setting, to the pattern of
Murder in the Cathedral. The elder statesman, Lord Claverton, retired and at the point of death, has given his life
to a social role, and is a hypocrite in the original sense, a

masked actor whose real life is in his *persona*. A weak spot in his self-sufficiency is indicated by his possessive attitude toward his daughter Monica and his son Michael. Two people out of his past, an Oxford chum now named Gomez, a low type who takes ice in his whisky, and a former mistress, Mrs Carghill, turn up in the role of accusing spirits, reminding him of previous misdeeds. The woman tells him, quoting a friend, that he has been kept from real vice, like Baudelaire's *lecteur*, not by virtue, but by the counter-vices of laziness and cowardice:

> "That man is hollow." That's what she said.
> Or did she say "yellow"? I'm not quite sure.

Their vampire-like professions of friendship ("I need you, Dick, to give me reality," Gomez says) suggest something almost demonic about them, as though the action were occurring in some waterless place after death—a suggestion intensified when another "sanatorium" opens up in the second act, run by a female who would be even more at home in hell than Harcourt-Reilly, as she keeps a television set in the "Silence Room." But Claverton's accusers are not demons, only self-justifying human beings, and they are, like Harry's Furies, instruments of grace. The elder statesman's *persona* breaks up and he confesses his misdeeds to Monica. They are not very black, probably because, as he says:

> It's harder to confess the sin that no one believes in
> Than the crime that everyone can appreciate.

This also reminds us of Harry, though the careful cleaning up of his past gives rather the impression of substituting a sentimental reality for a moral reality, to use terms from Eliot's essay on Heywood. There is also a good deal of talk about the relief following confession which sounds less like moral reality than like moral re-armament. Perhaps in his reaction the elder statesman underestimates the importance of the *persona*.

The denouement occurs when Michael goes off with the two accusers to start a new career. Michael symbolises a part of his personality that Claverton, assuming a double part, is ready to hand over to his tormentors: "For the *me* he rejected, I reject also." But he is not repudiating Michael: the fact that he is willing to see him begin a new life under Gomez' auspices, however unwillingly, is part of the annihilation of his ego. The rest is represented by Monica's marriage, a reminiscence perhaps of the conclusion of *Oedipus at Colonus*, where Antigone's desire to sacrifice herself for her father is gently thwarted. The elder statesman dies by himself, in the garden outside the sanatorium under a beech tree.

The dramatic monologues of Prufrock and Gerontion are studies of self-romanticising egos who are intermittently conscious of something more in their lives. Thoughts of the risen Lazarus and the martyred John the Baptist, witnesses to the power of Christ, float vaguely around Prufrock's brain. Gerontion, a more intelligent man, is more clearly aware of the "word within the word" and of the divine presence concealed in the bodies of his friends. These monologues are in a form of dramatic meditative verse in which a romantic illusion strangles a visionary conscience. In the comedies this form is turned inside out. Here we have a meditative drama in which we meet first a group of amiable but self-deceiving egos. They then form a hierarchy of enlightenment, from the hero or heroine at the top to a bewildered chorus below, a kind of epiphany of a spiritual élite.

Since the nineteen-twenties, critics have become increasingly aware of the continuity of the English Romantic tradition and of Eliot's place in it. The plays show the tension between Romantic and evangelical values that we should expect if we thought of Eliot as a poet in the main current of the English literary tradition, which runs through Milton and the Romantics. *Murder in the Cathedral*, with its sequence of temptations, is closer in conception to *Samson Agonistes* than to anything in Greek tragedy. Harry, prig or not, is as Byronic a figure as contemporary drama affords, and when another character in the same play says:

> And now I don't feel safe. As if the earth should open
> Right to the centre, as I was about to cross Pall Mall.

we are closer to Bunyan's interpreter's house than we are to the House of Atreus. The later comedies, with their alternately urbane and earnest texture, Sheridan crossed with John Wesley, reflect the same tension. One cannot both accept a tradition and decide what it is to be. For appreciating the real place of Eliot's drama, and perhaps his poetry too, in English literature, the amnesty proposed in "Little Gidding" does not go far enough. The greatness of his achievement will finally be understood, not in the context of the tradition he chose, but in the context of the tradition that chose him.

REFERENCES

1. Cp. Jer. *xxii*, 29; Isa. *xxxv*, 1; Ezek. *xxxvii*; Micah *vi*, 3; Ex. *xvii*, 6; Judges *xv*, 19.
2. Unger, p. 357.
3. "What is a Classic?" *O.P.P.* p. 70.
4. Cp. "Virgil and the Christian World," *O.P.P.* p. 131.
5. "Poetry and Drama," *O.P.P.* p. 84.
6. "Christopher Marlowe," *S.E.* p. 123.

BIBLIOGRAPHY

The following list was compiled with the help of *T. S. Eliot: a bibliography, including contributions of periodicals and foreign translations* by Donald Gallup, London (Faber) and New York (Harcourt) 1952.

Editions used as standard, where more than one exist, are marked *.

In Section II, *S.W.*, *F.L.A.*, *E.A.M.*, *S.E.* and *S.P.* indicate reprinting in *The Sacred Wood*, *For Lancelot Andrewes*, *Essays Ancient and Modern*, *Selected Essays* (1951), and *Selected Prose* respectively.

I. ELIOT'S POEMS AND PLAYS

Prufrock and Other Observations, London (Egoist) 1917.

Poems, London (Hogarth Press) 1919.

Ara Vos Prec, London (Ovid) 1920.

Poems, New York (Knopf) 1920. (Substantially the same as *Ara Vos Prec*.)

The Waste Land, New York (Boni and Liveright) 1922. (Reprinted, with the addition of notes, from *The Criterion*, I. 1 (Oct. 1922), pp. 50–64, and *The Dial*, LXXIII. 5 (Nov. 1922), pp. 473–85.)

Poems 1909–1925, London (Faber) 1925.

Journey of the Magi, London (Faber) 1927. (Ariel Poems no. 8.)

A Song for Simeon, London (Faber) 1928. (Ariel Poems no. 16.)

Animula, London (Faber) 1929. (Ariel Poems no. 23.)

Ash-Wednesday, New York (Fountain) and London (Faber) 1930.

Marina, London (Faber) 1930. (Ariel Poems no. 29.)

Triumphal March, London (Faber) 1931. (Ariel Poems no. 35.)

Sweeney Agonistes: fragments of an Aristophanic melodrama, London (Faber) 1932.

The Rock: a pageant play written for performance . . . on behalf of the Forty-Five Churches Fund of the Diocese of London, London (Faber) 1934.

Murder in the Cathedral, London (Faber) and New York (Harcourt) 1935.

Collected Poems 1909–1935, London (Faber) and New York (Harcourt) 1936.

The Family Reunion, London (Faber) and New York (Harcourt) 1939.

Old Possum's Book of Practical Cats, London (Faber) and New York (Harcourt) 1939.

East Coker, London (Faber) 1940. (Reprinted from *The New English Weekly*, Easter Number, 1940.)

Burnt Norton, London (Faber) 1941.

The Dry Salvages, London (Faber) 1941.

Little Gidding, London (Faber) 1942.

Four Quartets, New York (Harcourt) 1943, London (Faber) 1944.

The Cocktail Party, London (Faber) and New York (Harcourt) 1950.

* *The Complete Poems and Plays, 1909–1950,* New York (Harcourt) 1952.

The Confidential Clerk, London (Faber) and New York (Harcourt) 1954.

The Cultivation of Christmas Trees, London (Faber) and New York (Farrar) 1959. (Ariel Poems, New Series.)

The Elder Statesman, London (Faber) and New York (Farrar) 1959.

II. ELIOT'S PROSE

"Reflections on *Vers Libre,*" *The New Statesman,* VIII. 204 (3 Mar. 1917), pp. 518–19. *S.P.* (in part) pp. 86–91.

"Henry James," *The Little Review,* IV (Aug. 1918), pp. 44–53. Reprinted in *The Shock of Recognition,* ed. Edmund Wilson, New York (Doubleday) 1943, pp. 854–65; as "On Henry James" in *The Question of Henry James,* ed. F. W. Dupee, London (Wingate) 1947, pp. 123–33.

Ezra Pound: his metric and poetry, New York (Knopf) 1917.

"Whether Rostand had Something about Him," *The Athenaeum,* 4656 (25 Jul. 1919), pp. 616–17. Revised as "'Rhetoric' and Poetic Drama," *S.W., S.E.* pp. 37–42.

"Some Notes on the Blank Verse of Christopher Marlowe," *Art and Letters,* II. 4 (Autumn 1919), pp. 194–9. *S.W.* as "Notes on the Blank Verse of Christopher Marlowe": *S.E.* as "Christopher Marlowe," pp. 118–25.

"Tradition and the Individual Talent," *The Egoist,* VI. 4 (Sept.–Oct. 1919), pp. 54–5. *S.W., S.E.* pp. 13–22.

"Hamlet and his Problems," *The Athenaeum,* 4665 (26 Sept. 1919). pp. 940–1. (A review of *The Problems of "Hamlet",* by J. M. Robertson.) *S.W.: S.E.* as "Hamlet", pp. 141–6.

"Ben Jonson," *The Times Literary Supplement,* 930 (13 Nov. 1919), pp. 637–8. *S.W., S.E.* pp. 147–60.

"Swinburne," *The Athenaeum,* 4681 (16 Jan. 1920), pp. 72–3. Revised as "Swinburne as Poet," *S.W., S.E.* pp. 323–7.

"The Naked Man," *The Athenaeum,* 4685 (13 Feb. 1920), pp. 208–9. *S.E.* as "William Blake," pp. 317–22.

"Euripides and Gilbert Murray," *Art and Letters,* III. 2 (Spring 1920), pp. 36–43. As "Euripides and Professor Murray," *S.W., S.E.* pp. 59–64.

"Dante as a 'Spiritual Leader'," *The Athenaeum,* 4692 (2 Apr. 1920), pp. 421–2. *S.W.* revised as "Dante," pp. 159–71.

"Philip Massinger," *The Times Literary Supplement,* 958 (27 May 1920), pp. 325–6. *S.E.* as Part I of "Philip Massinger," pp. 205–15.

"The Old Comedy," in *The Athenaeum*, 4702 (11 Jun. 1920), pp. 760–1. *S.E.* as Part II of "Philip Massinger," pp. 216–20.

The Sacred Wood: essays on poetry and criticism, London (Methuen) 1920 and New York (Barnes & Noble) 7th ed., 1950.

"In Memoriam: Marie Lloyd," *The Criterion*, I. 2 (Jan. 1923), pp. 192–5. *S.E.* as "Marie Lloyd," pp. 456–9.

"The Function of Criticism," *The Criterion*, II. 5 (Oct. 1923), pp. 104–5. *S.E.* pp. 23–34.

"Four Elizabethan Dramatists," *The Criterion*, II. 6 (Feb. 1924), pp. 115–23. *S.E.* pp. 109–17.

Homage to John Dryden: three essays on poetry of the seventeenth century, London (Hogarth) 1924. (Contents: "John Dryden," "The Metaphysical Poets," "Andrew Marvell.") *S.E.* pp. 305–16, 281–91, 292–304.

"Lancelot Andrewes," *The Times Literary Supplement*, 1286 (23 Sept. 1926), pp. 621–2. *F.L.A.*, *E.A.M.*, *S.E.* pp. 341–53.

"Sir John Davies," *The Times Literary Supplement*, 1297 (9 Dec. 1926), pp. 906–7. *O.P.P.* pp. 132–7.

" 'Poet and Saint . . .'," *The Dial*, LXXXII. 5 (May 1927), pp. 424–31. Revised as "Baudelaire in Our Time," *F.L.A.* pp. 86–99, *E.A.M.* pp. 63–75.

"Thomas Middleton," *The Times Literary Supplement*, 1326 (20 Jun. 1927), pp. 445–6. *S.E.* pp. 161–70.

"Archbishop Bramhall," *Theology*, XV. 85 (Jul. 1927), pp. 11–17. As "John Bramhall," *F.L.A.*, *E.A.M.*, *S.E.* pp. 354–62.

"Introduction" to *Seneca His Tenne Tragedies* (1581), London (Constable) and New York (Knopf) 1927, pp. v–liv. *S.E.* as "Seneca in Elizabethan Translation," pp. 65–105.

Shakespeare and the Stoicism of Seneca, London (Oxford) 1927. (Address to the Shakespeare Association.) *S.E.* pp. 126–40.

"Bradley's 'Ethical Studies'," *The Times Literary Supplement*, 1352 (29 Dec. 1927), pp. 981–2. As "Francis Herbert Bradley," *F.L.A.*, *E.A.M.*, *S.E.* pp. 444–55.

"A Dialogue on Poetic Drama," *Of Dramatic Poesie, an Essay* (1668) by John Dryden, London (Etchells and Macdonald) 1928, pp. xi–xxvii. *S.E.* as "A Dialogue on Dramatic Poetry," pp. 43–58.

"The Humanism of Irving Babbitt," in *The Forum*, LXXX. 1 (Jul. 1928), pp. 37–44. *F.L.A.*, *E.A.M.*, *S.E.* pp. 471–80.

"Introduction" to *The Moonstone*, by Wilkie Collins, Oxford 1928, pp. v–xii (The World's Classics no. 316). As "Wilkie Collins and Dickens," *The Times Literary Supplement*, 1331 (4 Aug. 1927), pp. 525–6; *S.E.* pp. 460–70.

For Lancelot Andrewes: essays on style and order, London (Faber) 1928.

"Introduction" to *Selected Poems* of Ezra Pound, London (Faber) 1928.

"Second Thoughts on Humanism," *The New Adelphi*, II. 4 (Jun.–Aug. 1929), pp. 304–10. *S.E.* as "Second Thoughts about Humanism," pp. 481–91.

Dante, London (Faber) 1929. (The Poets on the Poets no. 2.) *S.E.* pp. 237–77.

Anabasis, by St-John Perse, with English translation by T. S. Eliot, London (Faber) 1930.

"Introduction" to *The Wheel of Fire: essays in interpretation of Shakespeare's sombre tragedies*, by G. Wilson Knight, London (Oxford) 1930, pp. xi–xix.

"Introduction" to the *Intimate Journals* of Charles Baudelaire, tr. by Christopher Isherwood, London (Blackamore) and New York (Random) 1930, pp. 7–26. *S.E.* as "Baudelaire," pp. 419–430.

"Cyril Tourneur," *The Time Literary Supplement*, 1502 (13 Nov. 1930), pp. 925–6. *S.E.* pp. 182–92.

"The Place of Pater," *The Eighteen-Eighties: essays by Fellows of the Royal Society of Literature*, ed. Walter de la Mare, Cambridge 1930, pp. 93–106. *S.E.* as "Arnold and Pater," pp. 431–43.

"Introductory Essay" to Samuel Johnson's *London: a poem, and The Vanity of Human Wishes*, London (Etchells and Macdonald) 1930, pp. 9–17. Reprinted as "Johnson's *London* and *The Vanity of Human Wishes*," in *English Critical Essays: twentieth century*, ed. Phyllis M. Jones, London (Oxford) 1933, pp. 301–10 (The World's Classics no. 405). *S.P.* (in part) pp. 163–9.

Thoughts after Lambeth, London (Faber) 1931. *S.E.* pp. 363–87.

"Thomas Heywood," *The Times Literary Supplement*, 1539 (30 Jul. 1931), pp. 589–90. *S.E.* pp. 171–81.

"Introduction" to *Pascal's Pensées*, tr. by W. F. Trotter, London (Dent) and New York (Dutton) 1931, pp. vii–xix (Everyman's Library no. 874.) As "The Pensées of Pascal," *E.A.M.*, *S.E.* pp. 402–16.

"Donne in Our Time," *A Garland for John Donne*, ed. Theodore Spencer, Cambridge, Mass. (Harvard) 1931, pp. 1–19.

Charles Whibley: a memoir, London (Oxford) 1931. (English Association Pamphlet no. 80.) *S.E.* pp. 492–506.

"John Ford," *The Times Literary Supplement*, 1579 (5 May 1932), pp. 317–18. *S.E.* pp. 193–204.

Selected Essays 1917–1932, London (Faber) 1932.

John Dryden, the Poet, the Dramatist, the Critic: three essays, New York (Holliday) 1932.

"Catholicism and International Order," *Christendom*, III. 11 (Sept. 1933), pp. 171–84. (Opening address to the Anglo-Catholic Summer School of Sociology.) *E.A.M.* pp. 113–35, *S.P.* (excerpt) p. 209.

The Use of Poetry and the Use of Criticism: studies in the relation of criticism to poetry in England, London (Faber) 1933 and New York (Barnes & Noble) 1955. (The Charles Eliot Norton Lectures [Harvard] for 1932–3.)

After Strange Gods: a primer of modern heresy, London (Faber) 1934 (The Page-Barbour Lectures at the University of Virginia, 1933.)

"John Marston," *The Times Literary Supplement*, 1695 (6 Jul. 1934), pp. 517–18. *S.E.* pp. 221–33.

Elizabethan Essays, London (Faber) 1934.

"Religion and Literature," *The Faith that Illuminates*, ed. V. A. Demant, London (Centenary) 1935, pp. 29–54. *E.A.M.*, *S.E.* pp. 388–401.

"Introduction" to *Selected Poems* of Marianne Moore, New York (Macmillan) 1935, pp. vii–xiv.

Essays Ancient and Modern, London (Faber) 1936.

"Modern Education and the Classics" (address to the Classical Club of Harvard, 1933). *E.A.M.*, *S.E.* pp. 507–16.

"Introduction" to *Poems of Tennyson*, London (Nelson) 1936, pp. ix–xix. *S.E.* as "In Memoriam," pp. 328–38.

"A Note on the Verse of John Milton," *Essays and Studies*, XXI (1936), pp. 32–40. *O.P.P.* as "Milton I," pp. 138–45.

"Byron" in *From Anne to Victoria: essays by various hands*, ed. Bonamy Dobrée, London (Cassell) 1937, pp. 601–19. *O.P.P.* pp. 193–206.

"Introduction" to *Nightwood* by Djuna Barnes, New York (Harcourt) 1937, pp. vii–xiv; London (Faber) 1950 (2nd English edition), pp. 1–7.

The Idea of a Christian Society, London (Faber) 1939 and New York (Harcourt). (Boutwood Foundation lectures, Corpus Christi, Cambridge.)

Christianity and Culture, New York (Harcourt) 1940.

"The Poetry of W. B. Yeats," *Purpose*, XII. 3–4 (Jul.–Dec. 1940), pp. 115–27. (The first annual Yeats Lecture to the Friends of the Irish Academy.) *O.P.P.* pp. 252–62.

"Introduction" to *A Choice of Kipling's Verse*, London (Faber) 1941, pp. 5–36. *O.P.P.* pp. 228–51.

The Music of Poetry, Glasgow (Jackson) 1942. (W. P. Ker Memorial Lecture, 1942: Glasgow Univ. Publications no. 57.) *O.P.P.* pp. 26–38.

The Classics and the Man of Letters, London (Oxford) 1942. (The Presidential Address to the Classical Association.)

"Johnson as Critic and Poet" (the Ballard Matthews Lecture, University College, North Wales, 1944), *O.P.P.* pp. 162–92.

"What is Minor Poetry?", *The Welsh Review*, III. 4 (Dec. 1944), pp. 256–67. *O.P.P.* pp. 39–52.

What is a Classic?, London (Faber) 1945. (Address to the Virgil Society.) *O.P.P.* pp. 53–71.

"The Social Function of Poetry," *The Adelphi*, XXI. 4 (Jul.–Sept. 1945), pp. 152–61. *O.P.P.* pp. 15–25.

"Milton," *Proceedings of the British Academy*, XXXIII (1947), pp. 61–79. (The Henriette Hertz lecture to the British Academy.) *O.P.P.* as "Milton II," pp. 146–61.

Notes towards the Definition of Culture, London (Faber) 1948 and New York (Harcourt).

The Aims of Poetic Drama, London (Galleon) 1949. (Presidential address to The Poets' Theatre Guild.)

"From Poe to Valéry," *Hudson Review*, II. 3 (Autumn 1949), pp. 327–42. (Lecture delivered at Library of Congress, 1948.)

"What Dante Means to Me," *Italian News*, 2 (Jul. 1950), pp. 13–18; reprinted in *The Adelphi*, XXVII. 2 (1st Quarter 1951), pp. 106–14. (Italian Institute lecture.) *S.P.* (in part) pp. 99–101.

Poetry and Drama, Cambridge, Mass. (Harvard Univ. Pr.) 1951. (The Theodore Spencer Memorial Lecture, 1950.) *O.P.P.* pp. 72–88.

* *Selected Essays*, London (Faber) 1951 (3rd English edition). (2nd U.S. edition, New York (Harcourt) 1950, includes everything but "John Marston.")

"Vergil and the Christian World," *The Listener*, XLVI. 1176 (14 Sept. 1951), pp. 411–12, 423–4. *S.P.* (in part) pp. 96–9, *O.P.P.* pp. 121–31.

Selected Prose, ed. John Hayward, Harmondsworth (Penguin) 1953.

The Three Voices of Poetry, London (Cambridge) 1953 and New York (Cambridge University Press) 1954. (National Book League annual lecture no. 11.) *O.P.P.* pp. 89–102.

American Literature and the American Language, St Louis (Washington Univ. Pr.) 1953. (An Address at Washington University.)

Religious Drama, Mediaeval and Modern, New York (House of Books) 1954.

"Goethe as the Sage" (address at Hamburg University, 1955, on receiving the Hanseatic Goethe Prize for 1954), *O.P.P.* pp. 207–27.

The Literature of Politics, London (C.P.C.) 1955. (Lecture at Conservative Political Centre.)

Essays on Elizabethan Drama, New York (Harcourt) 1956.

The Frontiers of Criticism, Minneapolis (Univ. of Minnesota) 1956. (The Gideon D. Seymour Lecture.) *O.P.P.* pp. 103–18.

* *On Poetry and Poets*, London (Faber) and New York (Farrar, Straus) 1957.

"Introduction" to *The Art of Poetry* by Paul Valéry, tr. by Denise Folliot, New York (Pantheon) 1958, pp. vii–xxiv. (Bollingen series no. XLV, vol. 7 of the Collected Works of Paul Valéry.)

III. SOME TITLES IN ELIOT CRITICISM

BEER, ERNST: *Thomas Stearns Eliot und der Antiliberalismus des xx. Jahrhunderts*, Vienna 1953. (Wiener Beiträge zur englischen Philologie, Bd. 61.)

BRAYBROOKE, NEVILLE (ed.): *T. S. Eliot: a symposium for his seventieth birthday*, London and New York 1958. (Essays by John Betjeman, Robert Speaight, etc.)

DREW, ELIZABETH: *T. S. Eliot, the Design of his Poetry*, New York 1949.

FREED, LEWIS: *T. S. Eliot: Esthetics and History*, La Salle, Ill. (n.d.).

GARDNER, HELEN: *The Art of T. S. Eliot*, London 1949 and New York 1959. (On *Four Quartets*.)

JONES, DAVID E.: *The Plays of T. S. Eliot*, London 1960.

KENNER, HUGH: *The Invisible Poet: T. S. Eliot*, New York 1959.

KENNER, HUGH (ed.): *T. S. Eliot: a collection of critical essays*, Englewood Cliffs, N.J. 1962. (Essays by R. P. Blackmur, William Empson, Ezra Pound, Allen Tate, etc.)

MACCALLUM, H. REID: "Time Lost and Regained" in *Imitation and Design*, Toronto 1953, pp. 132–61. (On *Four Quartets*.)

MARCH, RICHARD (comp.): *T. S. Eliot, a Symposium*, London 1948. (Essays by W. H. Auden, George Barker, etc.)

MARTIN, P. W.: *Experiment in depth: a study of Jung, Eliot and Toynbee*, New York (n.d.).

MATTHIESSEN, F. O.: *The Achievement of T. S. Eliot: an essay on the nature of poetry*, New York 1935. 2nd edition, revised and enlarged, 1947.

MAXWELL, D. E. S.: *Poetry of T. S. Eliot*, New York (n.d.).

MUSGROVE, S.: *T. S. Eliot and Walt Whitman*, New York 1952.

NOTT, KATHLEEN: *The Emperor's Clothes*, London and Bloomington 1953.

RAJAN, B. (ed.): *T. S. Eliot: a study of his writings by several hands*, London 1948. (Essays by M. C. Bradbrook, B. Rajan, etc.)

ROBBINS, ROSSELL HOPE: *The T. S. Eliot Myth*, New York 1951.

SEAN, LUCY: *T. S. Eliot and the idea of tradition*, New York (n.d.).

SMITH, GROVER: *T. S. Eliot's Poetry and Plays: a study in sources and meaning*, Chicago 1956.

UNGER, LEONARD (ed.): *T. S. Eliot, a selected critique*, New York 1948. (Essays by Ezra Pound, I. A. Richards, L. Unger, Edmund Wilson, W. B. Yeats, etc.)

WHEELWRIGHT, PHILIP: "Pilgrim in the Wasteland" in *The Burning Fountain*, Bloomington 1954, pp. 330–64. (On *Four Quartets*.)

WILLIAMSON, GEORGE: *A Reader's Guide to T. S. Eliot: a poem-by-poem analysis*, London and New York 1955.

WILSON, F. A. C. C.: *Six Essays on the Development of T. S. Eliot*, London and New York 1948.

CAPRICORN TITLES